Diego Rivera

Mexican Muralist

by Jim Hargrove

 CHILDRENS PRESS®
CHICAGO

Rivera

PICTURE ACKNOWLEDGMENTS

Smith College Museum of Art, Northampton, Massachusetts—Frontispiece

Courtesy of The Detroit Institute of Arts—pages 6 (2 photos), 55 (top), 56, 59, 60 (2 photos), 61 (bottom), 76

Courtesy of The Detroit Institute of Arts, property of the State of Veracruz—page 30

Courtesy of The Detroit Institute of Arts, INBA © Dirk Bakker—page 55 (bottom)

Courtesy of The Detroit Institute of Arts, San Francisco Art Institute—page 57

Courtesy of The Detroit Institute of Arts, Lucienne Bloch—page 58 (bottom); Lucienne Block (detail)—page 58 (bottom left)

Courtesy of The Detroit Institute of Arts, Universidad Autómonada Chapingo—page 62 (2 photos)

The Museum of Modern Art—page 18

AP/Wide World Photos—58 (bottom right), 61 (top), 88

LIBRARY OF CONGRESS
Library of Congress Cataloging-in-Publication Data

Hargrove, Jim.
    Diego Rivera : Mexican Muralist / by Jim Hargrove.
        p.   cm. — (People of distinction)
    Summary: Examines the life and work of the Mexican artist who decided that his great purpose in life was to bring art to the masses through the medium of murals.
    ISBN 0-516-03268-2
    1. Rivera, Diego, 1886-1957—Juvenile literature.
    2. Painters—Mexico—Biography—Juvenile literature.
    3. Mural painting and decoration—20th century—Mexico—Juvenile literature. 4. Social problems in art—Juvenile literature. [1. Rivera, Diego, 1886-1957. 2. Artists. 3. Mural painting and decoration—Mexico. 4. Painting, Modern—Mexico. 5. Art appreciation.] I. Title. II. Series.
ND259.R5H3   1990
759.972—dc20
[B]
[92]   89-25453
                                                      CIP
                                                       AC

398611

Table of Contents

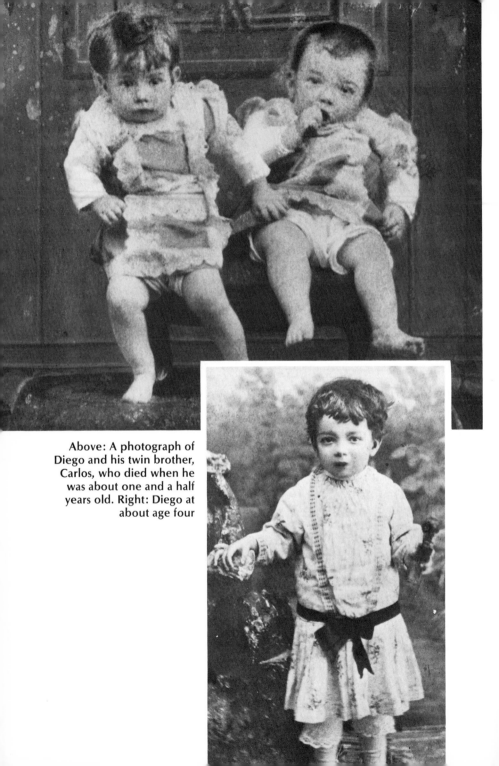

Above: A photograph of Diego and his twin brother, Carlos, who died when he was about one and a half years old. Right: Diego at about age four

Chapter 1

DRAWING TROUBLE

The city of Guanajuato was once a place where miners could become millionaires. It is nestled in a warm valley in central Mexico that is surrounded by mountains. There the widest and deepest veins of silver in all of the republic were once hidden below the surface of the hills that encircle the town.

Since silver was discovered in the area in 1550, Spaniards, Mexicans, and prospectors from all over the world dug pits and deep shafts and long tunnels there. It was all part of the endless search for the precious metal that lay buried under the sun-baked ground of Guanajuato.

Silver seemed to be everywhere. Not so very long ago, tiny bits of it could even be found in the mud and straw bricks, sometimes called adobe, that were used to make many of the town's older buildings.

More than a century ago, during the 1880s, Diego and María Rivera lived in a three-story building on narrow Pocitos Street near the middle of Guanajuato. The couple eventually became the parents of the most famous, and controversial, Mexican artist of the twentieth century.

Like many others, Diego and María Rivera hoped to

become wealthy by investing in silver mines. But even more than a century ago, the silver around Guanajuato was mostly gone. After buying interests in a number of mines with Spanish names such as *Los Locos* (the Madmen), *La Trinidad* (the Trinity), and *Mina de Jesús y María* (the Mine of Jesus and Mary), the couple was left with little silver but plenty of debts.

Other residents of the city had similar experiences. Some decided to leave. Diego and María stayed, the husband finding work as a schoolteacher, as an editor of a little newspaper, and soon as a local government official. Throughout most of the 1880s, when the Riveras lived at 80 Pocitos Street, Guanajuato was a sad little city. Only its older residents could remember the days when fortunes could still be made there.

Diego and María had other reasons for sorrow. During the years after their marriage in 1882, they tried to start a family. Three times María became pregnant. Three times her babies were born dead. After each misfortune, Diego bought a little doll for her. He knew that the toys were poor substitutes for a real child. The small gifts were all that the husband could think of to bring some comfort to his unhappy wife.

Late in the year 1886, María was pregnant again. On December 8, most of the residents of Guanajuato were celebrating one of the many religious festivals observed by Mexico's Roman Catholic church. That evening, the townspeople brought lighted candles into the local church building as a symbol of their religious faith.

Doña Cesaría, Diego's older sister, normally would have joined the faithful carrying candles to the little church. Tonight, however, she stayed in the house at 80 Pocitos Street instead. There were others inside as well: Diego, probably pacing the floor nervously; a doctor, who was also a family friend; and María, lying in bed. She was in labor for the fourth time in four years of married life.

When the time finally came, Diego stepped out of the room and waited. Because of the Rivera's unhappy experiences, he must have expected bad news to come soon. But at last he heard the cry of an infant. A little while later, Doña Cesaría emerged from the bedroom.

"Is it alive?" Diego nervously asked her.

"They're both alive," Cesaría answered.

Diego could hardly contain his joy. Both mother and baby had lived through the ordeal of birth. "Both?" he continued. "A boy?"

"Two!" Cesaría answered. "Two boys, two *hombres*, two sons, both, both alive. Two little baby boys!"[1]

It was a joyous moment. On December 8, 1886, the formerly childless couple suddenly was blessed with not one, but two little boys.

"I, the older, was named Diego after my father," Diego

said much later in a book about his life, "and my brother, arriving a few minutes later, was named Carlos. My whole name actually is Diego Maria de la Concepción Juan Nepomuceno Estanislao de la Rivera y Barrientos Acosta y Rodriguez."[2]

Fortunately, in later years Diego Rivera did not have to use all of his names when he signed his famous works of art. On his early pieces he wrote the names Diego María Rivera, to distinguish himself from his father while the elder Rivera was alive. Later, he simply signed them Diego Rivera.

For a time, the birth of twin sons brought great joy to the Rivera household. Unfortunately, the happiness was brief. When he was only one and a half years old, Diego's twin brother, Carlos, became sick and died. Faced with yet another tragedy, María grew sick at heart. Night and day, she stayed beside her dead child's grave. Her husband had to rent a room in the home of a cemetery worker in order to be near her.

The Rivera's family doctor began to fear that the young mother might go insane. He suggested that she find some work to keep her mind off her troubles. The elder Diego Rivera, and some of the family's relatives, urged her to return to school to study for a new career. María agreed, and eventually became a licensed midwife. In the meantime, the studies in school helped take her mind off the death of Carlos.

For a time, young Diego's life seemed to be in danger as

well. In his autobiography, a book called *My Art, My Life,* Diego described his early years of poor health:

"At two years old, according to photographs and the tales of my father and mother, I was thin and had rickets," he said. "My health was so poor that the doctor advised that I be sent to the country to live a healthy, outdoor life, lest I die like my brother.

"For this reason, my father gave me to Antonia, my Indian nurse. Antonia, whom I have since loved more than my own mother, took me to live with her in the mountains of Sierra.

"Antonia's house was a primitive shack in the middle of a wood. Here she practiced medicine with herbs and magic rites, for she was something of a witch doctor. She gave me complete freedom to roam in the forest. For my nourishment, she bought me a female goat, big, clean, and beautiful, so that I would have milk fresh from its udders.

"From sunrise to sunset, I was in the forest, sometimes far from the house, with my goat who watched me as a mother does a child. All the animals in the forest became my friends, even dangerous and poisonous ones. Thanks to my goat-mother and my Indian nurse, I have always enjoyed the trust of animals—a precious gift. I still love animals infinitely more than human beings."[3]

In his autobiography, Diego claimed that he lived with Antonia in the forest from the age of two until he was four years old. But in some of his other writings and conversations, he made no such claims. In all probability, he exaggerated his time there. In his later years, and perhaps in his earlier ones as well, Diego Rivera seemed to enjoy telling a tall tale or two.

In at least one aspect of his life, it is almost impossible to exaggerate. From a very early age, Diego showed signs of tremendous artistic talent. In 1889, well before his third birthday, he used a pencil and paper to draw a picture of a train, complete with a steam engine and a caboose. The drawing was saved by his mother, and it still exists in a Mexican museum. For an adult, the picture is not remarkable. For a two-year-old child, it is astonishing.

"One of my earliest memories of my youth," he once said, "is that I was always drawing."[4] Apparently, he was always drawing on just about everything. His pictures decorated the walls of his home, his furniture, even his parents' important paperwork, such as bills and record books. Soon enough, his father found a way to let him continue drawing while saving the family home from further destruction.

The elder Diego set up a room in the house in which his son could draw on anything, including the walls, the floor, and the furniture. The walls of the little art studio were covered with blackboards, so that old drawings could be erased to make room for new ones. Little Diego Rivera drew on the walls of his studio as a youngster, and on many more walls in his adult life.

For such a young boy, Diego showed surprising skill as an artist. But even during his earliest years, he began to prove that he had not one, but two utterly remarkable talents. His second great ability frequently eclipsed even his obvious gift for artistic expression.

Diego Rivera was a genius—an absolute master—at the art of making people angry! As an adult, he sometimes carried loaded pistols and wore a *bandolera* stuffed with bullets. Still, he almost always avoided physical violence. But he somehow found ways to make people so angry that they wanted to strangle him. From the age of three until the end of his life, he seemed to take great pleasure in it.

One of the first people to notice Diego's gift for making people angry was his great-aunt Vicenta. Like the other women in his family, Vicenta was very religious. She made sure that she attended the masses and all the festivals of the Catholic church. Unfortunately, she was never able to bring young Diego along. His father, who was opposed to the Catholic church, would not allow it.

One day, however, when Diego was three or four years old, his father was out of town. Great-aunt Vicenta made the mistake of taking the boy to church. Diego described what happened next:

"On entering the Church, my revulsion was so great that I still get a sick feeling in my stomach when I recall it. I remember examining the wooden boxes with their slots on top for the coins, then the man at the door in his long, dirty smock, collecting more money in a tin plate. There were paintings all around of women and men sitting or walking on clouds with little winged boys flying above them.

"In my own house, I had inspected my aunts' images of the Virgin Mary and Jesus Christ. I had scratched them and discovered that they were made of wood. I had put sticks into their glass eyes and through their ears to discover whether they could see, hear, or feel anything—always, of course, with negative results."[5]

The young artist stayed beside his aunt, who was kneeling in the church, but he could not remain quiet. He muttered that the older women and men surrounding him were idiots. Great-aunt Vicenta scolded him in a hushed but stern voice, and for a few minutes he was quiet.

For a time, he must have thought quietly about religion and the Catholic church. He must have wondered how some people could pray to pictures of Jesus or Mary, asking the pictures for things like pesos (a unit of Mexican money). Suddenly he could stand it no longer. To the astonishment of the worshipers, he dashed to the very front of the chapel and climbed up the wooden stairs to the altar.

"Stupid people!" he shouted from the high platform. "You reek of dirt and stupidity! You are so crazy that you believe that if I were to ask the portrait of my father, hanging in my house, for one peso, the portrait would actually give me one peso. You are utter idiots. In order to get pesos, I have to ask someone who has pesos to spare and is willing to give some to me.

"You talk of heaven, pointing with your fingers over your head. What heaven is there? There is only air, clouds which give rain, lightning which makes a loud sound and breaks the tree branches, and birds flying. There are no boys with wings nor any ladies or gentlemen sitting on clouds."[6]

It was quite a speech. According to Diego himself, who was known to exaggerate at times, it went on a good deal longer. He claimed that he stopped only after some of the worshipers began screaming, made the sign of the cross, and rushed out of the church calling him Satan. But something like that must have happened. Friends and neighbors were astounded by Diego's ability to speak in long sentences and paragraphs. And the episode at the church created a scandal that was remembered in Guanajuato for a long, long time.

Perhaps surprisingly, the young boy was not without defenders. The Catholic church, especially during Diego Rivera's time, was more controversial in Mexico than in many other countries. Some of its critics suggested that the church spent much of its energy defending the interests of wealthy people against the poorer classes. Some also felt that the Catholic church developed more of a sense of superstition and magic than true spiritual thought.

Diego's outburst in the place of worship created many enemies for such a young boy. But it also brought him support. That same night, as he was getting ready for bed, three elderly men came to visit him. Years earlier, the three men had all served as soldiers and had helped defend Mexico during a war. The three men were also wholeheartedly opposed to the Catholic church.

When little Diego came out of his front door to greet his visitors, the men removed their hats. The oldest, a man with an elegant white mustache, made a long speech. He said that he and the two others with him represented eleven freedom fighters from the city. He said that they were a brotherhood of veterans who now battled for freedom and the rights of men. He congratulated the young boy on his bravery and invited him to become their younger brother. He also pointed out that Diego's father and his grandfather were members of the same fraternity.

"Not one of us has ever used the freedom of speech and thought inside of the house of religion itself!" the old man said. "We congratulate you, young wolf. Will you shake hands and join us?"[7]

From that day until he was six years old and his family left Guanajuato, the little boy learned much about controversy. Many pious fingers were waggled at him, and the tongues of the religious faithful often clucked long after he had passed by. But he was also welcomed to sit on special park benches with the proud old veterans and a few other freethinkers at any time he wished.

From his earliest years to his last, Diego followed his fiery emotions and his sometimes unpopular beliefs wherever they led him, in his art and in his life as well. The two soon became inseparable.

Chapter 2

LEARNING ABOUT LIFE AND ART

Diego was five years old on the day his baby sister was born. One of his aunts was helping María with the delivery. The aunt assumed that the new baby would be a boy. Unfortunately, she decided that it would be best to hide the details of birth from her nephew.

"Look, Diego," his aunt said to him, "a little brother is coming for you today. I must go home because your mother isn't well. You go to the station to wait for him."[1]

Diego was happy to go to the railroad station. He was fascinated by trains, and had already talked some of the local engineers into allowing him to ride in their locomotives. But today was different. All day he waited impatiently at the station for a passenger train bringing his new brother. None was due until nightfall, and no train arrived unexpectedly.

The ticket agent, a family friend, finally told the boy toward evening that a sister had already arrived for him. The baby was sent to the Rivera's house in a fancy box, he said. Diego rushed home, wondering how his brother could have become his sister while traveling in a box.

When he saw the newborn baby, he declared that she was

ugly. Then he demanded to see the box that she was delivered in. His aunts frantically searched through the house, finally producing on old shoe box.

"You have told me many lies," Diego said as he examined the dusty box. "Now I know that my little sister did not come in a train or in a box. They gave mother an egg, and she warmed it in bed."[2]

The adults all laughed at the little boy's statement. They made jokes about a child being hatched from an egg, like a chicken. Furious that he was the subject of jokes, Diego stomped off to bed without eating dinner.

A few days after his sister was born and named María, Diego's mother found him trying to cut open the stomach of a pregnant mouse. He was, he said, trying to find out where little mice came from.

"My mother became hysterical," Diego remembered years later. "She cried out that in giving birth to me she had whelped a monster. My father also scolded me. He told me of the pain I had caused the mouse in cutting her up alive. He asked if my curiosity was so strong that I could be indifferent to the sufferings of other creatures. To this day, I can recall the intensity of my reaction. I felt low, unworthy, cruel, as if I were dominated by an invisible evil force. My father even started to console me."[3]

Over the next few weeks, Diego's father brought his young son medical books with illustrations that showed how human babies were born. Almost immediately, the boy began drawing pictures of people and animals, in addition to trains and toys, his usual subjects.

Problems for the Rivera family gradually mounted in Guanajuato. Among many of the townsfolk, Diego was already regarded as a nuisance at best, and as the very devil himself at worst. His father also was having difficulties.

In addition to his other jobs, the elder Diego edited a little newspaper called *El Democrata* (*The Democrat*). Some of his articles grew increasingly critical of the way the poor people in Mexico were treated. Noting that rates of poverty and illiteracy were high, he called for broad changes in Mexican schools and society.

Many of the family's neighbors began to regard both the father and his son as troublemakers. The debts mounting from the Riveras' worthless investments in silver mines also created financial problems. In 1892, when Diego was six years old, his mother decided to leave the city of his birth.

While her husband was working out of town, she sold all but a few of the family's belongings. With little Diego and one-year-old María, she traveled to Mexico City, a journey of about two hundred miles. She left word with neighbors that she was going to visit relatives. When her husband returned home and learned the news, however, he immediately understood that her move was meant to be permanent. He quickly followed his family to Mexico's capital city.

With little money, the family had to settle into a much smaller home in a poor neighborhood of Mexico City. To little Diego's dismay, the house had too few rooms to allow one to be set aside as his art studio. Gone as well was the nearby train station he adored, his elderly friends in the fraternity of freedom fighters, and the hills of Guanajuato, so much fun to explore.

Even back in 1892, Mexico City was huge. Thousands of people were moving there each year. Soon its population would swell to more than a million. Like Guanajuato, Mexico City was surrounded by mountains. But the mountains were much farther away and far less inviting.

Diego was unhappy for the first few years in his new city. For a time, he stopped drawing entirely. He became terribly ill, contracting first scarlet fever, then typhoid, and then diphtheria—all serious diseases. His great-aunt Vicenta helped nurse him back to health. She read to him stories from the books in his father's large library. She also let him examine her collection of Mexican folk art.

The little wood carvings, clay and ceramic sculptures, jewelry, and other items in Great-aunt Vicenta's collection were hardly regarded as great art by most educated people. But little Diego loved all of them, especially those with Indian designs. Throughout his adult life, he was fascinated by the ancient art of Mexico, a style developed before the arrival of European conquerors in the 1500s.

When the family first moved to Mexico City, Diego Rivera, Sr., had to settle for a low-paying job in the government's department of public health. Gradually, however, his fortunes improved. After living in the impoverished *barrio* (neighborhood) for more than two years, the family was able to move to a better home in a slightly wealthier area on the north side of the city.

At about this same time, Diego's mother gave birth to a boy, Alfonso, who lived just over a week. The unfortunate baby was at the center of a weird story about Diego. It was told by his sister María to the author Bertram D. Wolfe, who became a friend of the artist in later life and wrote an important book about him. According to the story, the family placed Alfonso's body in a tiny coffin on top of a piano.

"There," Wolfe wrote, "Diego found it while the adults were in another room. He and his sister proceeded to 'play house' with the waxlike corpse. Their games, beginning in mutual joy, always ended in open warfare. In a few moments María was screaming at the top of her lungs. The sound brought the grown ups into the room to find brother and sister tugging at the dead child! The scandal is still a shuddering memory in the family; to Aunt Cesaría, gruesome confirmation of her hypothesis that 'Diego was a devil in the form of a man'—and María not much better."[4]

The little devil finally overcame his overwhelming desire to move back to Guanajuato. In 1894, at the age of eight, he announced that he wanted to attend school. His parents had been waiting for that decision. His father, especially, was reluctant to send him until he declared himself ready.

"At eight I entered my first school," Diego said in his autobiography, "the Colegio del Padre Antonio. This clerical [religious] school was the choice of my mother, who had fallen under the influence of her pious sister and aunt. Except for a French teacher named Ledoyen, a former officer of the French army and a communist, there was nobody and nothing in the school that I liked, and I left it after a few months.

"I was next sent to another clerical school, the Liceo Católico Hispano, conducted by an intelligent priest, Father Servine. Here I was given good food as well as free instruction, books, various working tools, and other things. I was put in the third grade, but having been prepared well by my father, I was soon skipped to the sixth grade."[5]

Diego was an excellent student. A report card from December 1896 showed that he received first prize in the year-end exams. Late in 1898, he was graduated with honors from elementary school, just four years after entering. Only his training in Christian religious matters, a usual part of the school curriculum, was lacking. Priests at the school suggested he complete his religious training at home after he asked pointed and embarrassing questions about religious miracles.

Even before finishing elementary school, at his insistence, Diego began attending night classes at the San Carlos School of Fine Arts. For two grueling years, from 1896 to 1898, he learned reading, writing, and arithmetic by day, and basic principles of drawing and art at night. He was still enrolled in the San Carlos night school when he finished his elementary classes.

In order to get him enrolled in San Carlos, his parents were forced to mislead school officials about his age. For years, Diego was the youngest student at the art school. Nevertheless, he competed easily with the older students.

In 1898, after taking night classes for two years, Diego won second prize in the school's drawing program. The prize was a box of oil paints, which he used to draw landscapes. Soon afterward, he was awarded a scholarship that enabled him to take the school's regular day courses.

Even before his teenage years, Diego was already a superb artist. His pencil drawing entitled *Head of a Woman* was completed in 1898, when he was only eleven or twelve years old. The beautiful sketch shows his superb ability clearly and has been carefully preserved at the National Institute of Fine Arts in Mexico City.

The picture also shows that young Diego Rivera was drawing his works of art in much the same way that European masters had for centuries. The pencil sketch was refined and highly realistic, almost like a photograph. Over the years, he gradually moved away from that style.

Including his first two years of night courses, Diego attended the San Carlos School of Fine Arts for six years, from 1896 to 1902. During that time, he resigned himself to hard work, even though far too many of the courses were boring. For the most part, his classes emphasized technical skill and a rigorous study of nature. During this period, he received a number of small grants from the Mexican government.

"Among the teachers at the San Carlos," he said in his autobiography, "three stand out in my memory. The first was Felix Parra, a conventional painter himself but possessed with a passionate love for our pre-Conquest Indian art. He communicated this enthusiasm to me with such success that it has lived on in me, through many changes of taste and fortune, to this day.

"The second was José M. Velasco, whom I regarded as the world's greatest painter of landscapes. From Velasco, I learned the laws of perspective, and it was he, rather than Parra, whom I followed when I studied on my own. I traveled up and down the country, painting Indians, forests, houses, streets, and churches, all more or less in the manner of this master."[6]

The third teacher he remembered especially well was Santiago Rebull, who had once been the student of a famous French painter. Rebull stressed that the essence of painting was drawing. Under his instruction, Rivera developed even further his considerable ability at drawing lines and shapes. In his autobiography, Diego bragged about the time Rebull invited him to his studio, a place forbidden to all other students for twenty years.

Diego always said that his greatest teacher was not a member of the San Carlos faculty. He was not even a highly regarded artist at the time. His name was José Guadalupe Posada.

Posada worked in a small shop near the art school. On his way to and from afternoon classes, Diego began stopping by the little store to peer through the window. The things he saw inside were not even considered works of art by most people, but they fired his artistic imagination nevertheless.

Mexico was then, as now, a relatively poor country, especially compared to its wealthy neighbor to the north. Many Mexican people had little formal schooling and were unable to read or write. In the days before radio, motion pictures, and television, people who were unable to read were often entertained and informed about the news of the day by traveling singers and speakers. These wandering performers have been variously called troubadours, minstrels, and balladeers. Although they once roamed the world, they have all but disappeared today.

In the little shop where José Guadalupe Posada worked, songs and poems were printed on sheets of colored paper.

The pages were purchased by balladeers who carried them to their performances on street corners and in public squares throughout much of the republic. To make the sheets more interesting, Posada engraved drawings into the metal plates that were used to print the pages.

Diego Rivera was fascinated by Posada's illustrating. It was a different kind of art than he had ever seen before, sort of a cross between cartoons and standard art. The drawings also showed a strong influence of traditional Mexican Indian designs. Before long, Posada and Rivera became friends, and the young student spent many hours in the older man's shop, watching him work and discussing everything imaginable. Diego once said: "Posada taught me the connection between life and art—that you cannot paint what you do not feel."[7]

Compared with so much of the rest of his life, Diego's years at the art school seem unusually quiet and free from turmoil. But it was merely the calm before yet another storm.

By 1902, he began objecting to the school's emphasis on classical European art. He yearned to explore the folk art of Mexico. At the same time, he became increasingly aware of the corrupt practices of Mexico's dictator, Porfiro Díaz. Using a minor school scandal as an excuse for action, he helped organize a student strike. The students were actually protesting against the rule of President Díaz and the school's increasingly conservative courses.

"The student demonstration turned into a riot," Diego explained later. "As its leader, I was summoned before the authorities and expelled.

"Thus ended my formal training in art. Aside from a period of eight months in later years, when I was invited back to the San Carlos as its director, I would have no further connection with any academy.

"I was sixteen at the time I left the art school, the age when most students are first admitted."[8]

An oil painting completed in 1909, *Portrait of Angeline Beloff*, the Russian painter who became Rivera's common-law wife.

Chapter 3

SEEING THE WORLD

He was not quite a full-grown man, but at the age of sixteen Diego's student days were over. His huge body disguised his youthful age. By the time he was twenty, he was more than six feet tall and weighed three hundred pounds. He had large, bulging eyes, a wide forehead, and unruly black hair. Some people considered him ugly, but others found his exotic looks and lively behavior intriguing.

Officials at the San Carlos school invited him to return soon after he was thrown out. Instead, he began carrying his art supplies through the Mexican countryside from dawn to dusk, painting everything that interested him. As with any artist beginning his trade, he found it extremely difficult to earn money. He was able to sell a handful of paintings, but the prices were always low.

The lack of money caused problems for him. Among wealthy families in Mexico, parents often expected students to complete their educations in Spain. Although the Rivera family was by no means rich, a number of people began suggesting Diego should travel to Europe as well. Among them was Teodoro A. Dehesa, the governor of the state of Vera Cruz. Dehesa had helped arrange for a small scholarship for Diego, but it was far too little to pay for a trip abroad.

Another man who encouraged him to work and study in Spain was Gerardo Murillo, an artist who had spent much time there himself. Murillo was best known for his paintings of Mexican volcanoes. In a few years, he began calling himself Dr. Atl, an Aztec name meaning "water." Unfortunately, an eye disease left him nearly blind. Dr. Atl was unable to paint any longer, but many young artists in Mexico looked up to him. Among the admirers was Diego Rivera. "Atl fired me with the desire to go to Europe,"[1] he said.

In 1905, when he was eighteen years old, Diego told Governor Dehesa of his desire to travel. Dehesa replied that if Diego could sell his paintings at a one-man exhibition in Mexico, he would help underwrite his expenses. With great excitement, the artist spent a year and a half preparing paintings for the exhibit.

"When I had enough paintings," Diego said years later, "Atl organized my exhibit, I not being then, or ever since, capable of handling such practical affairs. Atl invited critics, writers, and newspapermen and, of course, potential buyers, sometimes using devious means to induce them to attend. The show went so well that everything, to the last sketch, was sold. I joyously reported this to Governor Dehesa, and he granted me the promised subsidy."[2]

During the winter of 1906-07, Diego celebrated his twentieth birthday and prepared to sail to Europe. During that time, however, he witnessed the cruelty of Porfiro Díaz, the dictator of Mexico.

For years, poor Mexican workers had toiled in the fabric mills of Vera Cruz. Their tiny wages were paid in coupons that could only be spent in company-owned stores. Many were whipped and beaten by mill bosses when even minor rules were broken.

By the winter of 1906-07, the workers decided to go on strike. Seeking help from President Díaz, the striking mill workers marched to his palace. After promising assistance, and without warning, the dictator ordered armed cavalry soldiers to attack the crowd. Men, women, and children were shot dead in the streets around the palace.

Apparently, Diego had been working in the area of the confrontation. In later years, he claimed that he took part in the battle, was wounded by a sword, and was finally thrown in jail. He never mentioned the incident earlier in his life, and it appears to be another of his tall tales. But the strike and its bloody aftermath were real enough. Diego never forgot the cruelty of Mexican president Díaz.

Filled with bitter memories of the strike, Diego sailed away for Spain, arriving on January 6, 1907. He brought along a letter from Dr. Atl that would introduce him to Eduardo Chicharro, a young but already well-known Spanish painter. Chicharro lived in the Spanish city of Madrid.

"As soon as I located Chicharro's studio," Diego remembered, "I set up my easel and started to paint. For days on end, I painted from early dawn till past midnight."[3] Throughout 1907 and 1908, he worked hard, usually under the direction of Chicharro.

After six months, Chicharro wrote an evaluation of his young student's efforts. Diego gleefully mailed the report to Governor Dehesa and a copy to his father. The Spaniard reported that the Mexican "Has made much progress, which I do not hesitate to qualify as astonishing. And therefore I am pleased to state that Señor Rivera, my pupil, shows that he has magnificent qualities for the art in which he is engaged, and . . . the qualities of a tireless worker."[4]

When he was not painting, Diego visited Madrid's world-renowned Prado Museum, where artworks by famous Spanish masters such as Goya and El Greco were displayed. He enjoyed looking at the old masterpieces, but, in general, his opinions of Spanish art and his own work in Spain were negative.

"My contact with Spanish art, however, affected me in a most unfortunate way. The inner qualities of my early works in Mexico were gradually strangled by the vulgar Spanish ability to paint. Certainly the flattest and most banal of my paintings were those I did in Spain in 1907 and 1908."[5]

At around that time, he began developing an increased awareness of the plight of poor people. He noted that many people, even those who worked long hours in Spanish factories, were impoverished. "Most of the common people were *picaros* or thieves," he claimed. "Having no legitimate ways of earning a living, they turned to lawless ones—rackets and crimes—in order to survive. They were shiftless, cunning, picturesque, sorrowful, and tragic."[6] Diego blamed the *Guardio Civil* (the police force run by the king) and the Spanish church for keeping working people unorganized and filled with despair.

Searching for answers, the young artist read dozens of books. Among the authors he admired was Karl Marx, whose books, written in the 1800s, helped lead to the creation of the first modern Communist government in Russia.

With thoughts of injustice and social reform beginning to fill his head, Diego decided to visit Paris in 1909. Many artists lived and worked here, and Diego must have wondered whether he should become one of them. With a friend, he took the train to Paris and rented a room at the Hotel Suez, where many Spanish and American art students lived. Later, he settled into the Hôtel du Suisse in the city's Latin Quarter.

At the time, Diego probably thought that he was only visiting Paris. But it immediately became his base of operations. Except for brief trips back to Mexico and visits to other European cities, Diego Rivera lived and worked in Paris for the next ten years.

One of the things that attracted him to Paris was the great number of art galleries. By walking up and down the streets of Paris, Diego could look into the windows of the galleries and see the paintings that were for sale inside. The best-known shops for modern paintings were along a street called Rue Lafitte.

Diego was particularly interested in finding paintings by Paul Cézanne. For a time, he had hoped to study under the famous French artist. Unfortunately, Cézanne had died a few years before Diego arrived in Paris. Still, the young man hoped to find a few paintings of the great artist.

One morning, Diego was walking along the Rue Lafitte when he spotted a Cézanne in the window of a gallery there. The gallery was owned by Ambroise Vollard, a respected but eccentric dealer who had taken an early interest in Cézanne. Diego was still looking at the painting at noon, when Vollard locked the shop and left for lunch. When the dealer returned about an hour later, he gave Diego an angry look and went inside.

Diego had little money and was dressed in shabby clothes. It was obvious that he could not afford to buy the valuable painting. But even as it started to rain, he just stood in front of the window, unable to take his eyes off the masterpiece. From time to time, Vollard looked at him angrily from inside the store. Suddenly the art dealer removed the painting from the window.

"I certainly did not look like a prospective customer," Diego recalled, "so Vollard at first must have decided I was a thief planning to break in and steal the painting. Otherwise, why would he have removed it from the window? Just as I was about to leave, he reappeared with a second and equally exciting canvas, which, without any indication of an awareness of my presence, he again placed before me. However, a few minutes later I could see my 'friend' watching me from inside. Nevertheless, I remained, for this new picture was just as tantalizing and challenging as the previous one. Finally, and perhaps in exasperation, he returned, removed this work, and substituted still another. Soon it seemed like a game. Fascinated, I stood moored before this window for the remainder of that rainy day while Vollard, now probably as intrigued by my behavior as I was by his, proceeded to remove and replace canvas after canvas. This, the equivalent of a private showing, was my first and marvelous introduction to the original paintings of Cézanne, Matisse, van Gogh, Renoir, and others."[7]

Midnight passed and the rain continued to pour, but Diego stood in front of the gallery. The dealer kept the shop open long after its usual hours. Finally, Vollard stopped changing the paintings. He came to the doorway and said, "*Vous comprenez, je n'en ai plus.*" ("You understand, I have no more.")[8] Diego continued studying the last painting. When he decided at last to leave, Vollard walked up to the doorway, probably intending to say something. Assuming that the dealer was angry, Diego walked quickly away.

In Paris, Diego did much work along the Seine River. He would set up his easel in the early morning and paint the scenes he saw throughout the day. Although he had little money, his life as an artist allowed him to do as he pleased, and so he decided to travel. During the summer of 1909, he traveled to Belgium, where he visited the ancient cities of Brussels and Bruges.

In Brussels, Diego ran into a young woman he had known in Spain, Maria Gutierrez Blanchard. Maria had a short, deformed body but a beautiful face. She would soon become known as one of the finest painters in Paris. With her was a friend, an attractive young Russian painter named Angeline Belloff. "Much to her misfortune," Diego joked, "Angeline would become my common-law wife two years later."[9]

Diego, Maria, and Angeline traveled to Bruges. There, Diego began one his best-known early paintings, *The House on the Bridge*. From the North Sea port at Bruges, the trio bought tickets on a small steamship that sailed to London. In the huge English city, Diego visited art museums and galleries. But he seemed most interested in London's enormous slums and the plight of the poor people who lived in them.

"At dawn," he observed, "the homeless and jobless overran the sidewalks to rummage through the garbage. Even these despairing people demonstrated the impeccable good manners of the English. No matter how hungry he appeared to be, I never saw an Englishman dip his hand into the waste can until all the women had had their turns. And every one of His Majesty's subjects observed the rule that he put his hand into it only once.

"I sometimes wondered why, on this kind of diet, the people of London didn't die at a prodigious rate. Then I discovered that there was actually a law, backed up by heavy fines, forbidding the mixing of waste food with any other kinds of waste. In other words, garbage cans were legally recognized as the free cafeterias of the vagrant and the poor."[10]

Diego Rivera brought his sketches and paintings, as well as his impressions of Europe's poor people, back to Paris in November 1909. For the better part of three months, he worked to complete his painting called *The House on the Bridge*. When it was finished, he submitted it to a jury of art critics. The critics decided it was good enough to be included in a major Paris exhibition. His friends congratulated him on his success, but Diego insisted that such acceptance was an insult. Nevertheless, he was pleased to see *The House on the Bridge* displayed in the huge collection of six thousand paintings.

The twenty-three-year-old artist was already getting his first taste of success, but he was also becoming homesick. Back in Mexico, he noted, probably with some bitterness, a huge celebration was being planned.

Porfiro Díaz, the dictatorial president of Mexico, was planning to celebrate his thirtieth year in office. As luck would have it, the event coincided with Mexico's one hundredth anniversary as an independent nation. As part of the festivities, the San Carlos School of Fine Arts was planning an exhibition and had invited Diego to submit his work.

In June 1910, the artist traveled back to Madrid, where he put the finishing touches on a number of canvases he planned to show at the San Carlos exhibit. In the early fall, he boarded a steamship bound for Mexico.

Diego Rivera returned to his homeland on October 2, 1910. He went to his parents' house in Mexico City, where his mother was stunned to see him. He had not told her that he was coming. Remarkably, on that same day his old Indian nurse, Antonia, appeared at the house without warning. She conducted a mystic ceremony and then disappeared.

Soon after Diego arrived in Mexico, a growing number of people were beginning an open revolt against the corrupt rule of Díaz. In support of the revolutionary spirit, Diego claimed that he made a poster that included these words: "THE DISTRIBUTION OF LAND TO THE POOR IS NOT CONTRARY TO THE TEACHINGS OF OUR LORD JESUS CHRIST AND THE HOLY MOTHER CHURCH."[11] Of course, his views about the Catholic church were by now well known. He was reacting against the church's role in maintaining the power of Mexico's ruling class.

On November 20, 1910, the very day that the San Carlos art exhibit opened, a presidential candidate named Francisco Madero declared that Díaz had stolen the recent election. Díaz had forced Madero to flee to the United States, where the politician called for civil war. Under the leadership of men such as Emiliano Zapata, Francisco "Pancho" Villa, and Pascual Orozco, peasant armies began to rise throughout much of the republic.

In Mexico City, the Díaz regime tried to pretend that nothing serious was going on. Díaz himself was planning to attend opening day of the San Carlos exhibit. At the last minute, however, he sent his wife instead. According to Diego, the president had learned that the artist and some of his friends were planning to blow him up with a bomb hidden in a paint box. There is little support for this claim from other sources.

Carmen Romero Rubio de Díaz, wife of the embattled president, officially opened the exhibit and purchased six of Diego's paintings. Other representatives of the Mexican government bought seven others. By the end of the first day, all but two of Diego's forty paintings had been purchased.

It was a smashing success for the young artist, but he suddenly had little interest in art. As the battles against the Díaz regime grew, he retired to the nearby state of Morelos and watched the action unfold.

The civil war was brief. Less than five months later, on

May 25, 1911, Díaz was forced to resign. Tragically, the new rulers of Mexico proved nearly as corrupt as the old ones. In June, Diego sailed to Cuba, and from there sailed back to Paris.

Chapter 4

PORTRAITS IN PARIS

Diego's passport was not entirely in order for his voyage back to Spain. Few questions were asked, however, when he boarded an aged ship called the *Alfonso Trece*. Due to bad weather, the trip to Europe took a week longer than scheduled. The rusty *Alfonso* was tossed like a toy on the heavy seas. Many of the passengers, and some of the crew, became seasick. For a time, Diego had to work in the ship's cargo hold to help redistribute the freight stored there. Otherwise, the bobbing ship might have capsized.

By September 1911, he was back in Paris. As soon as he arrived, he hurried to see Angeline Belloff, the woman he had met in Brussels through Maria Blanchard. "Both of us had agreed to wait until this moment to see whether our love was strong enough to withstand the test of separation," Diego remembered.

"We now decided to live together.

"For the next ten years that I spent in Europe, Angeline lived with me as my common-law wife. During all that time, she gave me everything a good woman can give to a man. In return, she received from me all the heartache and misery that a man can inflict upon a woman."[1]

There were days of great sadness ahead for both of them, and happy times as well. After visiting the Spanish city of Toledo, Diego and Angeline moved into a studio at 26 rue de Départ in the Paris neighborhood called Montparnasse. Many other painters and sculptors lived in the same quarter of the city. In fact, the entire block Diego and Angeline chose to live in was filled with artists' studios.

Diego had little trouble acting out his role as an eccentric artist. Like other painters of Montparnasse, he enjoyed spending an hour or two in the cafés of Paris. There, he met other artists, as well as writers and poets. Speaking in both Spanish and French, he seemed to enjoy telling shocking stories to the people gathered around him in the little cafés. Many people were astonished by the wild tales he told.

Often accompanied by Angeline and other friends, Diego visited Spain at least once a year during his ten-year stay in Paris. Even during his first trip there after his return to Europe in 1911, he began experimenting with a new kind of art that was sweeping Paris. By the year 1913, he was one of the leaders of the new artistic movement called cubism.

Throughout history, artists developed many different styles of drawing and painting. Almost all of them, however, showed the world in a more or less realistic way. When an artist painted a picture of a human being, for example, just about anyone, even a child, could recognize the subject as a person. Whether an artist painted an animal, an angel, a city street, or a bowl of fruit, it was generally quite easy to recognize.

Led by the artists Pablo Picasso, Georges Braque, and others, a number of painters who worked in Paris in the early years of the twentieth century changed all of that. For the first time, these cubist painters began creating art that, at least to average people, looked very odd.

In cubist paintings, familiar objects were often drawn in exaggerated geometric forms. A human face, for example, might take the shape of a triangle, or a cone. That same face might be separated from the rest of the head, the head itself drawn far from the shoulders. In the same painting, the strange face might be shown as it appeared from the front and from the side at the same time.

Many people who knew little about art, and even some who did, thought cubism was weird. But Diego Rivera was quickly drawn to it. From the years 1913 to 1917, Rivera completed about two hundred paintings in the cubist style.

"I have always been a realist," Diego said late in his life, "even when I was working with the cubists. . . . I believe this movement to be the most important single achievement in plastic art since the Renaissance. I also believe that my cubist paintings are my most Mexican."[2]

When another revolution was raging in Mexico, Diego painted his *Zapatista Landscape—The Guerrilla*. The cubist painting shows a guerrilla soldier standing in front of a range of mountains. The mountains, a rifle, a type of Mexican hat called a *sombrero*, and a Mexican cape are easy enough to see. But the soldier in the middle of it all is barely noticeable. The artist used the cubist technique, perhaps, to show how Mexican soldiers fighting against government troops had to remain nearly faceless in order to survive.

Even for an artist, Diego's life-style in Paris was unconventional. He always shared his studio with Angeline Belloff, and sometimes with her friend Maria Blanchard as well. When Angeline was away, housekeeping suffered. Both Diego and Maria refused to cook or clean. Maria claimed that once, when Angeline was away from Paris, a piece of beef remained on a plate in the studio for twenty days. It was finally discarded by a neighbor who objected to the smell.

The mess was not the result of laziness, exactly. Diego worked hard on his paintings, usually rising before dawn to begin work. Although he would often spend a few hours during the day visiting a café or the studio of a friend, he was often back at work in the evening.

Some of the people who posed for him remarked about his unusual working habits. Most artists insist that models remain motionless for hours on end, holding a carefully planned pose. Diego was just the opposite. His models could do as they pleased, even leave the studio to take a walk. Diego just kept on working as if nothing had happened.

He had a great many friends in Paris, many of them artists or writers. One was the famous Spanish painter and sculptor Pablo Picasso. "In a spirit of pure mischief," Diego said about his days with Picasso, "we would often play tricks on our women acquaintances, among whom I had acquired a terrible reputation.

"When one of them would come to his studio, Picasso would hide me behind a door. In the course of the conversation, Picasso would happen to mention my name."[3] At the mention of his name, Diego claimed, the woman would make all kinds of unkind statements. As he opened the door to show that Diego was right there, Picasso would say, "Well, *I* said he was an angel."[4]

An even closer friend was the Italian artist Amadeo Modigliani. Modigliani was a superb painter, a kind friend, and an alcoholic, almost always in need of money. Diego and Angeline often helped their unfortunate friend, but money soon became a problem for them as well.

In the early months of 1914, it seemed as if things were going well for Diego's career. From April 26 to May 6 of that year, he held his first and only one-man art show in Paris. Twenty-five of his works were shown, and many of them were sold. Of course, there was a scandal as well. In a printed catalog describing the exhibit, an attack was made on cubism. Art critics were outraged, but Diego made a handsome profit despite the flap.

In the summer, he traveled with Angeline, Maria, and some other friends to Spain. They intended to walk through the countryside, painting the sites they saw.

On June 28, shortly before they left, the archduke of Austria was assassinated by a student from Serbia (today a part of Yugoslavia). Within a few weeks, Austria declared war on Serbia, Russia declared war on Austria, Germany declared war on Russia and France and invaded Belgium, and Britain declared war on Germany. World War I had begun.

As all of this was happening, Diego and his friends reached the Spanish seacoast. There they saw an English warship firing at a German submarine. With a feeling of hopelessness, the travelers rode in a boat to the island of Majorca, where they stayed for three months. As some of his fellow travelers were drafted into various armies, Diego, Angeline, Maria, and the others remaining in the group headed back to the Spanish mainland. With very little money left, they stayed in the city of Barcelona.

Fearing that he would be killed in the war, Diego's mother and his sister rushed to Spain to see him one last time. Confronted by their surprise visit, Diego threatened to kill himself. Instead, he and Angeline sold everything they had so that his relations could purchase tickets for their passage back to Mexico.

As they were attempting to reenter France, Diego felt forced to enlist in the French army. He was turned down.

The rejection may have been because he was too fat, or because he had flat feet, or because of his strange political views. Any one of those reasons would have been sufficient.

He and Angeline were eventually able to return to Paris, where they remained for the duration of World War I. They were brutal years. Food, clothing, and heating fuel became increasingly scarce. During winter, the studio was almost unbearably cold. Like other artists living in Paris, Diego was forced to work even harder merely to survive. When he or one of his friends managed to sell a painting, a great celebration was held, and a little wine, bread, and cheese was shared by all.

During this period, Diego tried unusual experiments with his art. He mixed sand and other grainy substances with oil paints to give his drawings a different texture. He even tried painting with wax and plaster instead of oil. Instead of using traditional canvas, he sometimes drew on pressed cork and on other surfaces as well.

He also began talking with the Russian and Eastern European friends of Angeline Belloff. He became fascinated by Angeline's homeland. For years to come, the fascination increased with each passing season.

Early in the year 1916, Angeline informed him that she was going to have his baby. "If the child disturbs me," he said, "I'll throw it out the window."[5] His only son, named Diego, Jr., was born on August 11, 1916.

Diego didn't toss the baby out the window. Instead, in the spring of 1917, he decided to leave Angeline and live with another woman, named Marievna Vorobiev. Like Angeline, Marievna was a Russian painter living in Paris. About six months later, when he told her that he was going back to Angeline, Marievna attacked him with a knife. At least two years after that, she gave birth to a daughter. Diego, she said, was the father.

By most reports, especially Diego's, Marievna was a beautiful but unbalanced and violent woman. In his autobiography, Diego said that some of his friends felt sorry for her and "purchased many of her paintings to compensate her for the damages done to her by Rivera. She achieved similar results with sentimental American collectors. They began pestering me with appeals to repent and help her. Of course, I paid no attention to them. The child Marika, now grown up and married, is a lovely woman and an accomplished dancer. For many years, she too wrote me letters and sent me photographs in the hope of softening my flinty old heart. I never responded. The past was past. Even if, by the barest chance, I really was her father, neither she nor Marievna ever actually needed me."[6]

In that same autobiography, Diego didn't mention the many times he helped Marievna and Marika financially. Before he left Paris, he left money with a mutual friend for their assistance. For years afterward, he helped the mother and daughter meet expenses for illnesses and other emergencies, helped pay for Marika's schooling, and paid for her dancing classes. In the meantime, however, he went back to Angeline, who accepted his return with surprisingly little anger, even though he continued to see Marievna.

Throughout the year 1917, Diego's personal life, like the world at large, was in an uproar. World War I was still raging on bloody battlefields throughout much of Europe. In Mexico, civil war continued, with a new president taking power. In Russia, one historic revolution was followed by a second one.

Diego Rivera was particularly fascinated by the revolutions in Russia. By October 1917, armies whose leaders promised a new form of government and social order had seized power there. Gone, said the Russian Bolsheviks, were the days of unfair privilege and terrible poverty of old Russia. Leaders such as Vladimir Lenin promised a new society in which all Russians would share equally in the prosperity of the land.

To Diego Rivera, who had often noted the unfair differences between rich and poor in Mexico as well as in Europe, the words of the Bolshevik leaders were spellbinding. He and his friend Amadeo Modigliani applied for a visa to visit Russia, but both were turned down.

Near the end of the following year, 1918, World War I finally came to an end. But even before the final battles were fought, a personal tragedy struck Diego and Angeline. During a flu epidemic in the fall, Diego, Jr., became ill.

"Unfortunately," the father remembered, "the painting I was now doing found no buyers. Angeline and I were down and out. Our flat was bitingly cold. When our little son, born just before my affair with Marievna, became sick, there was no money for doctors or medicine or, for that matter, for food, and the baby died."[7]

Not long after his second birthday, Diego Rivera's only son was buried in Père Lachaise cemetery. Sadly, the parents decided to move out of the Montparnasse art district of Paris. For Diego Rivera, the end of an era was approaching.

Even before his son died, Diego had been quarreling openly with Picasso and other cubist artists. Around 1917, he stopped painting in the cubist style altogether. On his canvases he began to portray once again the realistic scenes familiar to classical painters. In 1918, he created a number of famous paintings, including *The Mathematician* and *Still Life with Ricer*. Neither work revealed even a hint of the cubist style.

His mind filled with the slogans of the Russian revolution, Diego Rivera was more interested in the life of the common man than in the views of the artists and art critics of Montparnasse. The common people didn't care for cubism. By now, neither did Diego Rivera.

Soon after the end of World War I, Diego became friends

with a doctor named Elie Faure. The artist and his older friend talked for hours. As a doctor, Elie Faure had seen the horrors of the war, but he also loved art and wrote poetry. Elie Faure kindled Diego's interest in a form of art called fresco.

Fresco painting is an ancient art, dating back thousands of years. To make a fresco, an artist uses special watercolors to paint on plaster while it is still wet. The plaster is often applied to walls or ceilings, frequently large ones. As it dries, a chemical reaction with carbon dioxide gas in the air takes place. Because of this reaction, the watercolors are covered with a thin layer of calcium, a crystalline mineral. The hard cover gives fresco paintings an unusual glow—and tremendous durability. Some fresco paintings that are more than three thousand years old are still perfectly preserved today.

Frescoes were painted by Mexican Indians before the arrival of Spaniards in the 1500s. But of all the countries in the world, Diego knew, Italy had the richest fresco treasures. In the ancient catacombs of Rome, early Christians had used frescoes to decorate burial vaults. In more-recent centuries, Italian painters such as Raphael and Michelangelo had created frescoes acclaimed throughout the world.

Diego decided to go to Italy. "To obtain the money I needed to live and travel," he said, "I turned to a brother Mexican, the engineer Alberto Pani, then serving as Mexican minister to France. Pani, who was later to figure in one of the great Rivera art scandals, bought my portrait, 'The Mathematician,' and commissioned portraits of himself and his wife. With the money I received from these, I went to Italy to study the frescoes of the old masters."[8]

Saying good-bye to Angeline, he left for a seventeen-month stay in Italy. He made hundreds of sketches of the great frescoes he saw, as well as scenes from everyday Italian life. From city to city, he traveled in third-class train seats. He slept at all hours on the trains, so that when he arrived at a new city he could spend more time exploring it.

By the summer of 1921, he had finally seen enough. At the age of thirty-four, his great purpose in life was now finally clear. It involved painting, of course, but not on canvases to be purchased by wealthy art collectors. And he would not use a hard-to-understand style like the cubists of Paris.

Diego Rivera would paint for the common folk, the masses of people on every continent who seldom could afford to buy paintings for themselves or find the time to visit a museum. He would paint for the world, with a clear style on huge walls for everyone to see. His radical politics, his desire for attention, and his fabulous skill all pointed together in this new direction.

It was time to go home.

Above: Rivera's parents, Diego, Sr., and Maria, on their wedding day in 1882

Left: *Zapatista Landscape— The Guerrilla* was painted in 1915. Around 1917, Rivera stopped painting in the cubist style.

Dr. Atl (with beard) and Rivera at the National Palace in about 1929

In *The Making of a Fresco, Showing the Building of a City,* Rivera even included himself, from the back, working on his fresco. It hangs today in the San Francisco Art Institute.

Murals created for the New Worker's school in 1933 were placed on movable frames so they would not be destroyed when the building was demolished.

There was great opposition to Rivera's murals in Rockefeller Center because he included a portrait of Lenin.

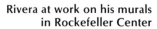

Rivera at work on his murals in Rockefeller Center

Above: the Rivera home in San Angel
Below: Rivera working on a mural in 1950

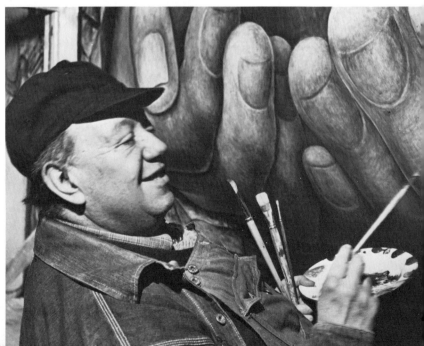

Left: In 1955 Rivera went to the U.S.S.R. for cancer treatment. He said he loved Moscow and sketched the walls of the Kremlin.

Below: Mourners crowd the entrance to the Palacio de Bellas Artes during Rivera's funeral in 1957.

The Chapingo panels depicted Rivera's Communist ideals. Two of the panels are named *Dividing the Land* (above) and *Good Government* (below).

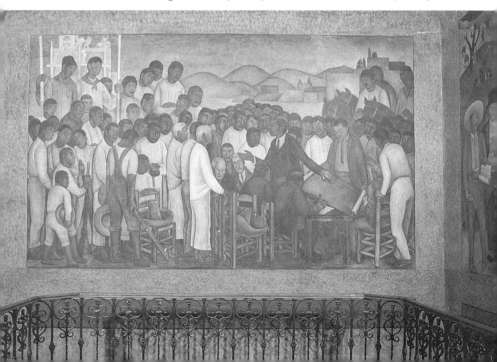

Chapter 5

WORLDS ON WALLS

His studies in Italy completed, Diego returned to Paris in June 1921. Soon after his arrival, he received a telegram bearing the sad news that his father was dying in Mexico. Quickly, he sold a number of pictures, said farewell to both Angeline and Marievna, and boarded a ship bound for his native land.

Since his last visit home a decade earlier, Mexico had been torn apart by political violence. In that brief span, the country's government was controlled by ten different presidents, with twice that many candidates battling for power. Diego must have hoped that the latest leader, General Álvaro Obregón, would bring some stability and peace to the troubled nation.

Mexico may have been in a crisis, but Diego's return in July filled him with wonder. "On my arrival in Mexico," he wrote, "I was struck by the inexpressible beauty of that rich and severe, wretched and exuberant land."[1]

"It was as if I were being born anew," he remembered at another time, "born into a new world. All the colors I saw appeared to be heightened; they were clearer, richer, finer, and more full of light. The dark tones had a depth they had never had in Europe. I was in the very center of the plastic world, where forms and colors existed in absolute purity. In everything I saw a potential masterpiece—the crowds, the markets, the festivals, the marching battalions, the workingmen in the shops and fields—in every glowing face, in every luminous child. All was revealed to me."[2]

The artist was thrilled that the first sketch he made back in Mexico turned out well. Many more followed. But for his first half year home, Diego was unable to pursue his dream of becoming a muralist, a painter of huge pictures on walls.

The government of General Obregón had the best of intentions, but was nearly bankrupt. Although Mexico's latest leaders wanted better schools, new hospitals, and improved services for its people, there was little money with which to work. Great plans were made and soon abandoned for lack of funds. Like others, Diego became involved in several doomed government programs.

He was hired briefly as director of the government's propaganda trains, although no one seemed to know exactly what a propaganda train was. Director Rivera quickly learned that most of the nation's railroad cars had been lost during the years of fighting.

Next, he became an art consultant for a government publishing house. The consultant retired without publishing a single book. He also served as the director of a school for workers that never opened.

Finally, in November 1921 came the break that started his career as a muralist. The government's minister of education, José Vasconcelos, invited Diego and a group of other artists and poets to tour several sites rich in ancient Mexican Indian artwork. Always fascinated by Mexico's early art, Diego enjoyed the outing enormously.

More important, however, the trip gave him an opportunity to talk at length with Minister Vasconcelos. He shared with the minister his dream of painting walls. By the start of the following year, the minister found him a wall to paint.

Diego was given the opportunity to paint his first mural on the inside front wall of the National Preparatory School auditorium. The building was part of the University of Mexico in Mexico City. By early 1922 he was already making sketches of the work, which eventually were enlarged to the mammoth size the mural would assume.

During the earliest stages of his work, he met a young woman from Guadalajara named Guadalupe Marín. Everyone called her Lupe. Diego was introduced to her by a popular singer of the day. At the first meeting, Lupe turned to the singer and asked, "Is *this* the great Diego Rivera? To me he looks horrible!"[3]

From that awkward beginning, a romance began. By everyone's account, Lupe was beautiful, cultured, and wild. Diego made many sketches of her, and included her image in some of his murals. In some of those pictures, he transformed the beautiful woman into an odd, sometimes even ugly, image. But Lupe seemed to enjoy them all.

In June 1922, while he was still working on the auditorium mural, Diego married Lupe in a Catholic church. Of course, church weddings were hardly his favorite events, especially when he was the groom. But Lupe insisted on it for the sake of her family. The newlyweds moved into a well-preserved old house near Mexico City's central square.

Diego worked on the auditorium wall throughout the year 1922. In many ways, the mural he created there differed from his later efforts. Instead of painting in fresco, he used an equally ancient system in which colors were combined with beeswax. The sticky mixture was applied to the wall and then sealed with heat.

"The subject of the mural was Creation," Diego explained, "which I symbolized as everlasting and as the core of human history. More specifically, I presented a racial history of Mexico through figures representing all the types that had entered the Mexican blood stream . . ."[4]

At the center of the mural, in an alcove built to enclose an organ, was the figure of a man with Indian features. He represented creation. To his left were nine women symbolizing various aspects of wisdom. To his right was a group of men representing the sciences. The figures surrounding the central man had mixed racial features.

The mural demonstrated Rivera's great skill as an artist,

but it hardly pointed in the direction he wanted to take his art. The ideas were far too abstract for his taste. He was still shaking off the influence of the Paris cubists and the classical painters of Italy. He had not yet found his own style. Even before the mural was finished, he grew dissatisfied with it.

The wall did, however, attract considerable attention. Young artists, intrigued by an art form they had not seen before, started gathering in the auditorium to watch Diego work. Many of them began to assist him. Before long, much of Mexico City was talking about the project. Whether the mural was good art or bad, a worthwhile project or a waste of time and money, were topics of conversation almost everywhere.

Mexico's minister of education had mixed emotions about the mural, but he knew what his country could afford. The Obregón administration did not have the money to pay for the new schools and hospitals it wanted to build. But it certainly could manage to pay the low wages even well-known artists such as Diego Rivera commanded. For relatively little money, the public buildings of Mexico could be made beautiful! At the same time, the works of art could be used to portray the history and dreams of a nation in which most people were still unable to read.

To meet the challenge of beautifying Mexico, Diego and a number of his fellow artists organized a kind of trade union called the Syndicate of Technical Workers, Painters, and Sculptors. A number of its members, including Rivera, José Orozco, David Siqueiros, Xavier Guerrero, and fifteen-year-old Máximo Pacheco, were, or soon became, well-known artists and muralists.

In a statement about its goals, members of the union criticized "the so-called easel painting and all the art of ultra-intellectual circles, because it is aristocratic and we glorify the expression of Monumental Art because it is a public possession." With that said, members of the union began seeking work painting government buildings.

"We applied for and received work under financial arrangements identical to those of house painters," Diego said. "Soon frescoes blossomed on the walls of schools, hotels, and other public buildings . . ."[5]

While all this was happening, Diego was in the disappointing final stages of his first mural. Around the time he finished it, he decided to join Mexico's Communist party. At various times in recent years, many other prominent Mexicans had done the same. A majority, at least among government officials, had already quietly dropped out. Some people were beginning to believe that communism was not the answer to poverty. But Diego kept his faith in the fair-minded slogans of the Russian revolution.

The Communist party in Mexico was in decline when Diego decided to take up its cause. *El Machete* (*The Sword*), a newspaper published by Rivera and other members of the Syndicate of Technical Workers, Painters, and Sculptors, soon became the official publication of Mexico's Communist party. Over the next few years, Diego was never too busy or too poor to give the party at least some of his time and quite a lot of his limited money. Free time, however, was soon hard to find.

As soon as he completed his work on his first project, the minister of education hired him for a second and even larger task. With a number of other painters from the recently created union, he was hired to decorate the walls around a huge open-air courtyard in the headquarters of the Secretaría de Educación Pública (the Ministry of Public Education). The recently built structure was just a block or two from the auditorium he had worked on before.

"For several months before beginning my work in this government building," Diego said, "I roamed the country in search of material. It was my desire to reproduce the pure, basic images of my land. I wanted my paintings to reflect the social life of Mexico as I saw it, and through my vision of the truth, to show the masses the outline of the future."[6]

As Diego's friend and biographer Bertram D. Wolfe pointed out, it is difficult to imagine the size of the project. The courtyard was three stories high, two city blocks long, and one block wide. A series of 124 frescoes would be painted along the walls, with a total area of more than

17,000 square feet. If the paintings were somehow placed end to end and squeezed to the height of this book, they would be more than four miles long.

Because of his growing fame, political connections, and endless work, Diego soon took over the entire job from the artists who began working with him. Few others had the talent, and none had the energy, to compete with him. In the face of open competition, the spirit of brotherhood briefly enjoyed by the members of the Syndicate of Technical Workers, Painters, and Sculptors quickly disappeared. So, eventually, did the union itself.

In the courtyard of the Ministry of Public Education, Rivera perfected the technique of fresco painting that made him famous throughout the Western world. He began by making pencil sketches of each scene in his studio. When he was satisfied, he enlarged the drawings to the size of the final fresco.

Now much of the work was handed to assistants. Skilled masons applied several coats of plaster to the area of wall being readied for the new art. Diego took great care in specifying plaster that met his exacting standards. To make it, lime had to be heated over a wood fire, processed for three months, and shipped in rubber bags to keep out moisture. When all but the final layer was applied to the wall, his aides then traced the lines of the full-size sketches with a sharp tool, digging the outlines into the plaster. Late at night, a final, thin coat of lime mixed with marble dust was spread over the outline. When this smooth layer was firm, but not dry, it was time to get the maestro out of bed.

At dawn, Rivera arrived at the courtyard. His assistants were already busy grinding pigments by hand, and then mixing the colored powders with distilled water on a slab of marble. When he judged the thick paints to be just right, Diego scraped them onto a plate and climbed the scaffold to begin his work. He must have considered fresco painting dangerous, because he usually wore a holstered pistol and a bandolera well stocked with bullets.

Quick and accurate work was necessary. The final layer of plaster would remain damp for only six to twelve hours, depending on the weather. Once dry, the plaster would no longer absorb paint in the proper way. When the air was hot and parched, masons had to prepare new surfaces constantly. Diego worked all day, as long as there was enough light to see. Artificial light could not be used, because it would alter the appearance of the colors.

For days, months, and finally years, Diego toiled on the scaffolds around the courtyard walls. Huge crowds of people gathered to watch him work. All stayed a safe distance away. Few dared to disturb such a well-armed artist! As daylight completely faded into night, Diego climbed down for a final look at the day's work. Sometimes, it just wasn't good enough. "Clean it all off and put on fresh plaster!" he would order his assistants. "I'll be back tomorrow morning at six."[7]

Because the architecture of the Ministry of Education building was complex, no photograph can show the full majesty of Rivera's work there. Only details of individual frescoes can be captured by a camera. Diego did, however, describe his work in various parts of the elaborate courtyard:

"The work of the people that I depicted in the Court of Labor was weaving, cloth-dyeing, farming, and mining. As in life, the workers' lot is not easy: I showed the miners, for example, entering a mine in one panel and emerging in the adjacent panel, weary and exhausted. . . . In one fresco, I painted a rural school teacher at her noble work while armed peasants stood guard . . .

"In the court of Fiestas, I represented a contrasting mood of Mexican life. Here, the people turned from their exhausting labors to their creative life, their joyful weddings and their lively fiestas. . . . In addition, I depicted what could become a great source of happiness for the Mexican Indian if it could but be realized—scenes showing the self-sufficiency of the *ejidos*, the land given the Indian to farm."[8]

Like the laborers he painted in his frescoes, Diego was a tireless worker. Although he was paid the equivalent of only two American dollars a day, he rarely stopped painting as long as there was enough light. During the final years of his work on the Ministry of Education courtyard, he found relaxation by starting another set of murals. He was hired to paint frescoes in the administration building and the chapel at the Universidad Autónoma de Chapingo (the Agricultural College at Chapingo).

In his paintings at the Chapingo school, Diego displayed his Communist ideals even more strongly than in the courtyard frescoes he was completing at the same time. He gave his Chapingo panels titles such as *Good Government, Bad Government, Dividing the Land, Birth of Class Consciousness, Formation of Revolutionary Leadership,* and so on. At the same time, he began including revolutionary slogans on some of his courtyard frescoes.

Communism was not hated as much then in Mexico as it is today in America. But Diego's radical politics created an uproar nevertheless. Some Mexicans who took pride in their light skins wondered why so many of the artist's drawings were of dark-skinned people. Some critics said that his figures were crudely drawn. A growing number called for the artworks to be destroyed. Even before he began work on the school at Chapingo, political changes were working against him.

In December 1924, a new chief executive came to power in Mexico. Aides of new president Plutarco Elías Calles were no friends of Diego Rivera or of his radical art. Right after the election, an assistant to the president-elect told Bertram

D. Wolfe, "As soon as Calles is President, his first official act will be to rub off those ugly monkeys of Diego's from the walls of the Secretariat."[9]

In the end, it was the very people Rivera despised most who saved his art. Wealthy art lovers and critics from Paris, New York, London, and much of the world traveled to Mexico City to look at his controversial frescoes. Whatever the politics of the painter, they said, the paintings were clearly masterpieces. No one in the Mexican government cared to be remembered as the one who destroyed the celebrated works of Diego Rivera.

By August 1927, Rivera had completed the Chapingo murals and nearly all of the more than one hundred panels at the Secretaría de Educación Pública. He had created a body of work that would take many artists a lifetime to finish. He was already famous, and becoming ever more so.

And his personal life was in a shambles.

Although he was certainly fat and considered ugly by many, his talent and colorful behavior attracted women like a magnet. Some followed him to work in the morning and home at night. The boldest actually climbed onto his scaffold to personally express their love and desires.

Diego's art was strong but his flesh was weak, at least when it came to women. His wife Guadalupe suffered through his nearly continuous absence while working. She felt the sting of poverty made far worse by his unending contributions to the Communist party. In the midst of it all, she gave birth to two daughters. The first was named, like herself, Guadalupe, and soon nicknamed Pico. The second was named Ruth, and called Chapo.

For a time, Lupe endured her husband's absence and his string of infidelities. But she was not the kind of woman to suffer forever. She began regarding her husband with bitterness.

Once, while working on the Chapingo murals, Diego fell asleep and slipped off his scaffold. He was brought home unconscious. "Throw him on the couch in the corner," Lupe ordered. "I'll tend to him when I have finished my dinner."[10] Although a doctor discovered that his skull was cracked, he eventually recovered. His marriage to Lupe, however, did not survive. Husband and wife separated in July 1926.

When he finished the Chapingo murals a year later, Diego Rivera was already both famous and infamous. But the greatest controversies of his life were still ahead.

Rivera painting in Detroit in 1933

Chapter 6

COMRADES IN ART

Four days after he completed the murals for the agricultural college at Chapingo, Diego went to Russia. With a group of other Communist leaders from Mexico, he was invited to attend the Moscow celebrations of the tenth anniversary of the October Revolution. Ten years earlier, in October 1917, Lenin, Trotsky, and other Communists took control of the government of Russia.

On his way across Europe by train, Diego stopped in Berlin, the capital of Germany. There he saw a young politician named Adolf Hitler give a fiery speech in front of the headquarters of the German Communist party. Hitler eventually came to power as an anti-Communist. At the time, however, he worked with Communists.

When interpreters told him what Hitler was saying, the artist suggested that the German politician should be killed. When no one volunteered, Diego supposedly offered to do it himself. "Let me shoot him, at least," he claimed to have said to his German hosts. "I'll take the responsibility. He's still within range."[1] In his autobiography, Diego maintained that the people with him merely laughed, saying that Hitler was a harmless idiot.

The story is probably another of the artist's tall tales. There is no doubt, however, that he saw early and clearly the danger posed by the Nazi party.

Diego and the other Communists traveling with him arrived in Moscow in the fall of 1927. At first, the artist was impressed by his Russian hosts, and they by him. He was in the only country on earth with the kind of government he glorified in his art. His hosts were surprised and flattered that he spoke some Russian. He had picked it up in Paris from Angeline Belloff and her Russian friends.

As a visiting dignitary, he was able to watch outdoor events from the reviewing stand near the Kremlin building, the center of Russian government. He drew sketches of the Red Army as it passed by in a colorful parade. On November 24, he signed a contract to paint a fresco in a building called the Red Army Club. As an even greater honor, he was asked to paint a portrait of Joseph Stalin, the premier of Russia.

Although his visit started out well, trouble came soon enough. His first sketch of Stalin was hardly flattering. He became ill during the cold Russian winter and was hospitalized, delaying his start on the murals in the Red Army building. In February, he gave a speech at a Moscow academy in which he declared what was wrong with Russian art. He found plenty of things to complain about.

Russian government leaders regarded art as propaganda. In other words, they used it to explain the theories of communism and to further its goals. The best-known artists in Russia were told what subjects to paint and how to paint them. Those who refused to do what they were told, including some people Diego had known in Paris, all but disappeared. In his speech, Diego pointed out that most of the nation's officially approved art was bad.

On the other hand, he praised Russian folk art, especially the types of religious works called icons. "Look at your icon painters," he said, "and at the wonderful embroideries and lacquer boxes and wood carvings and leatherwork and toys. A great heritage which you have not known how to use and have despised!"[2]

It was not the kind of speech the Russian government wanted to hear. Like Diego Rivera, the Communist leaders had little use for religion. Unlike the artist, however, they were unwilling to accept any kind of art that did not serve their political plans.

Within a few more months, Russian officials had seen enough of Rivera. Arrangements were made with the Communist party of Mexico to call him home. He returned to Mexico on June 14, 1928.

For the rest of his life, Rivera said that his commitment to communism remained unchanged. Little more than a year after his return to Mexico, however, he was tried, convicted, and thrown out of the Communist party. For all but the final year of his life, he was attacked by party members at almost every opportunity. They charged that he was disloyal, undisciplined, and unwanted.

The reaction of Communist party officials against Rivera is hard to understand. More than any other artist then or now, he illustrated in his monumental murals what were supposed to be the principles of communism.

"Mexican muralism—for the first time in the history of monumental painting—ceased to use gods, kings, chiefs of state, heroic generals, etc., as central heroes. . . . " Diego said. "For the first time in the history of art, Mexican mural painting made the masses the hero of monumental art. That is to say, the man of the fields, of the factories, of the cities, and towns."[3]

Back home in Mexico, Rivera seemed far more in tune with the lives of working people than the Communist bosses in Moscow. Unfortunately, his native land was once again in turmoil.

General Álvaro Obregón, who had served as president of Mexico from 1920 to 1924, had recently been reelected. In July 1928, President-elect Obregón was assassinated. An interim president was installed in office, but outgoing President Plutarco Calles continued to control the government behind the scenes. Early the following year, a Cuban Communist staying in Mexico named Julio Mella was murdered as well, this time on orders of the Cuban government.

Because it was strictly anti-Communist and wished to

avoid an international incident, the government run by Calles decided to ignore the involvement of Cuban assassins. Instead, they charged Mella's girlfriend, Tina Modotti, with the murder.

Diego knew Tina well and considered her a friend. He was outraged at the false charges against her. So were other members of Mexico's Communist party. As his last official party act, Rivera helped defend her in court, presenting considerable evidence of Cuban involvement in the murder of Julio Mella. As the case unfolded, men working for ex-President Calles threatened to kill Diego. Nevertheless, he and Tina Modotti were victorious.

"As for Calles," Diego remembered afterward, "he was later kicked out of power by my good friend, Lázaro Cárdenas, recent President of Mexico. With appropriate civilian and military rites, he [Calles] long ago descended into hell. . . ."[4]

While political turmoil in Mexico swirled around him, Diego was given a great honor. In April 1929, he was named director of the San Carlos School of Fine Arts, the same school that had once expelled him. There was another honor as well. Soon after he was threatened with death by government agents, he was asked to paint murals on the walls of the Palacio Nacional. The National Palace was perhaps the most famous building in Mexico, housing the offices of the president, the treasury, and other government agencies.

For thirteen turbulent months, Director Rivera shook the

San Carlos school to its very foundation. He completely altered the curriculum, demanding that students work in factories by day and attend art classes only at night. Each student would follow this discipline for eight years, the director decided. After that, the best students could study art both day and night. In May 1930, dazed school officials finally managed to force Rivera from office.

In July 1929, while still serving as the San Carlos director, he began work on his murals in Mexico City's National Palace. Serving as the nation's Capitol, the building is situated in the Plaza de la Constitucion. On this historic site, the Aztec Indian emperor Montezuma held court in his own magnificent palace five centuries ago. Here too was the headquarters and home of the Spanish conqueror Hernando Cortés, who defeated the Aztecs and founded Mexico City.

Rivera understood perfectly well the historic significance of the Capitol building and the Plaza de la Constitucion. Along the Capitol's great stairways, he planned his most ambitious work yet: a huge illustration of the entire history of Mexico.

"For the wall of the right staircase," he said, "I envisioned Mexico before the Conquest: its popular arts, crafts, and legends; its temples, palaces, sacrifices, and gods. On the great six-arched central wall, I would paint the entire history of Mexico from the Conquest through the Mexican Revolution. At the triangular base, I would represent the cruelties of Spanish rule, and above that, the many struggles of my people for independence. . . . The four central arches would show aspects of the Revolution against Diaz and its reverberations in the strife-torn years of [Presidents] Madero, Huerta, Carranza, Obregón, down to the ugly present of Plutarco Calles."[5]

All of these visions and more were realized in a series of magnificent frescoes created during the years 1929 and 1930. But as if a thorough history of his nation was not enough, Rivera also planned to depict the future of Mexico along a nearby wall. This vision too was completed, but not until 1935. In the meantime, he was interrupted by a series of projects that made headlines throughout the United States and much of the world. Even earlier, he made a much-needed change in his chaotic personal life.

On August 21, 1929, Diego Rivera got married—for the third time in his own mind, for the second time in his native land, and for the first time according to Mexican law. Although his marriage to Lupe had been in a church, the pair had not signed the legal documents the republic of Mexico required to recognize a marriage.

The August 23 edition of *The New York Times* included an Associated Press story under headlines reading:

DIEGO RIVERA MARRIES
Noted Mexican Painter and Labor Leader Weds
Frida Kohlo[6]

The AP story twice misspelled the maiden name of Diego's bride, Frida Kahlo. Soon, her correct name would become far better known by a great many Americans. In the meantime, however, Diego had found a wonderful companion. The nineteen-year-old girl was a talented artist, just like her forty-two-year-old husband. She had been a mischievous student in school and a member of the Young Communist League.

In the Communist party, members tend to call each other "comrade." But it was Frida, more than anyone else, who became Diego's greatest comrade until her death in 1954.

According to Diego, he first saw Frida when she was a mop-haired schoolgirl and he was painting his first mural. For hours, she sat and watched him work in the National Preparatory School auditorium. Then she delighted in hiding out in the dark corners of the big room, shouting out warnings when any of his various lady friends came near.

As a teenager, she was involved in a terrible automobile accident. Her spinal column was cracked, her pelvis broken in three places, and a leg and a foot badly injured. Not expected to live, she spent a year flat on her back in a body cast. With only her arms free to move, she taught herself how to paint.

When she had finally healed enough to walk, she gathered up her paintings and brought them to the Ministry of Education building, where Diego was then at work. "Hey, Diego, come down here,"[7] she hollered to the artist on the scaffold. The older man was impressed by the younger woman's work. Soon he visited her home and looked at all her odd, strikingly original paintings. Before long, she was posing for some of his murals.

"You have a dog-face," Diego told his new model.

"And you have the face of a frog!" she answered.[8]

And so, of course, they soon faced married life.

After his marriage, Diego continued working on his already famous frescoes at the National Palace. Soon there was a new assignment. The United States Ambassador to Mexico, Dwight W. Morrow, hired him to paint murals in a building called the Palacio de Cortés. The Palace of Cortés was, and still is, in the town of Cuernavaca just south of Mexico City. After the frescoes there were completed on November 7, 1930, Ambassador Morrow gave them to the people of Mexico.

Within a couple of days after the Cuernavaca murals were finished, Diego and Frida Rivera were on their way to the United States. Diego had been hired to paint a mural in the Luncheon Club of the new Pacific Stock Exchange building in San Francisco. An offer made to him several years earlier for a smaller fresco in the California School of Fine Arts also was still open.

Because of his Communist background, Diego had tremendous difficulty getting a visa permitting him to enter the United States. Only the help of a wealthy California businessman with friends in the U.S. State Department made his visit possible. To add to the insult, Communists around the world hooted at a so-called revolutionary painter who was working for millionaire stockbrokers.

Despite the obstacles, the Riveras' stay in the beautiful city on the Pacific Ocean was very pleasant. "We were welcomed magnificently by the people of San Francisco," Diego recalled, "and were feted at parties, dinners, and receptions. I received assignments to lecture at handsome fees."[9]

As with any monumental work by Rivera, there were a few controversies. But compared with those of the past, and in contrast to the storm that would soon come, the squabbles were minor and all in good fun.

His mural at the stock exchange was called *Allegory of California.* Most of its scenes showed miners, farmers, prospectors, engineers, and other working people. The workers were depicted making good use of the state's priceless natural resources. At the mural's center was the head and shoulders of a young woman. The artist used her as the "Symbol of California."

The real-life model was Helen Wills Moody, a popular tennis player. When it was unveiled on March 31, 1931, most people were enormously impressed by the fresco. A few thought it unfair that one tennis player had the honor of symbolizing an entire state.

Near the end of his visit in San Francisco, Diego also completed a relatively small fresco at the California School of Fine Arts (today the San Francisco Art Institute). The mural showed a number of planners, architects, and workers involved in the construction industry. In the foreground, it also included a wooden scaffold and artists at work painting the mural itself.

The Making of a Fresco, Showing the Building of a City, appeared to be a mural on top of a mural. The artist even included a picture of himself, from the back, working on his fresco. Most people agreed it was a lovely mural and a clever idea. The only problem, a few people whispered, was at its center. There Diego Rivera's chubby fanny seemed to dominate the picture. A critic suggested it was the artist's way of insulting the city.

Diego insisted that no offense was intended. But it hardly mattered. The amusing controversy paled in comparison with the white-hot drama to come.

Rivera and Frida in Mexico City in 1939

Chapter 7

THE ARTIST WINS THE BATTLE OF DETROIT BUT LOSES THE WAR IN ROCKEFELLER CENTER

During much of the time Diego and Frida were in San Francisco, Ortiz Rubio, the newly elected president of Mexico, sent letters and telegrams demanding the artist's return to Mexico City to complete the National Palace murals. On June 8, 1931, the Riveras flew home. Within a week, Diego was working again on the frescoes at the National Palace.

Using the money he earned in California, Diego hired workers to build a home and adjoining studio for himself and Frida in a Mexico City neighborhood called San Angel. Diego's fame as both an artist and a colorful character was helping him, for the first time in his life, earn reasonably high fees.

Near the end of the year, the Museum of Modern Art in New York City began the second one-man show in its brief history to showcase the art of Diego Rivera. Nearly fifty-seven thousand people attended the month-long exhibit, a record for the museum, which had been founded just two years earlier. Already, however, plans were being finalized for an even greater event.

Back when he was painting in California, Diego was

visited by the director and another official of the Detroit Institute of Arts. Detroit was then, and remains today, the center of the automobile manufacturing industry in the United States. Fascinated by the industrial machinery he saw in America, Diego told the museum officials about his desire to create a mural celebrating machines. In the great, clanking engines of American industry, Rivera saw the possibility of liberating the working masses from much of their drudgery.

The head of Detroit's art commission was Edsel Ford. Edsel's famous father, Henry Ford, had created the first mass-produced cars in America. Edsel Ford agreed to contribute ten thousand dollars to pay for a series of frescoes Rivera would paint in the central courtroom of the Detroit Institute of Art. Before long, when Diego insisted on painting more than had originally been planned, Edsel graciously increased his contribution to twenty-five thousand dollars.

On April 21, 1932, Diego and Frida arrived in Detroit. They began living in a hotel directly across from the Institute of Arts. Diego met immediately with members of the Detroit art commission, and plans for the new mural were finalized. But he did not begin the actual work for some time.

"I spent two and one-half months between my meeting with the Art Commission and the beginning of my actual mural work in soaking up impressions of the productive activities of the city," he said. "I studied industrial scenes by night as well as by day, making literally thousands of sketches of towering blast furnaces, serpentine conveyor belts, impressive scientific laboratories, busy assembling rooms; also of precision instruments, some of them massive yet delicate; and of the men who worked them all. I walked for miles through the immense workshops of the Ford, Chrysler, Edison, Michigan Alkali, and Parke-Davis plants. I was afire with enthusiasm. My childhood passion for mechanical toys had been transmuted to a delight in machinery for its own sake and for its meaning to man—his self-fulfillment and liberation from drudgery and poverty."[1]

Diego also traveled to nearby Greenfield Village. There Henry Ford had built a huge indoor and outdoor museum displaying the history of American technology. After Diego began working on the frescoes, he had a personal meeting with Henry Ford himself. The artist judged the millionaire manufacturer to be "a most charming man, old in years but in other ways very young. Discarding formalities, Ford greeted me with a hearty handshake and then began one of the most intelligent, clever, and lively conversations I have ever enjoyed."[2]

In his autobiography, Rivera admitted to a bit of embarrassment about his feelings for Henry Ford. "I regretted that Henry Ford was a capitalist and one of the richest men on earth," he said. "I did not feel free to praise him as long and as loudly as I wanted to, since that would put me under the suspicion of . . . flattering the rich. Otherwise, I should have attempted to write a book presenting Henry Ford as I saw him, a true poet and artist, one of the greatest in the world."[3]

It was an odd situation. A Communist painter, who had long complained bitterly about the abuses of wealth and power, was now working for one of the richest families in America. Soon he received word that other wealthy Americans were anxious to hire him as well. John D. Rockefeller, Jr., perhaps the richest man in the world, was considering employing him to decorate the lobby of his RCA (Radio Corporation of America) Building, a part of the enormous Rockefeller Center complex then under construction in New York City. Top executives at General Motors also were interested in acquiring their own Rivera fresco.

Diego worked on the Detroit frescoes throughout the second half of 1932 and the early months of 1933. During that time, both he and Frida had problems with their health. Diego went on a severe diet of mostly citrus fruits and juices. He lost a hundred pounds and most of his energy. (Three years later, a doctor ordered him "reinflated and not disinflated again under any circumstances."[4]) Frida became pregnant but suffered a miscarriage at Detroit's Henry Ford Hospital. Doctors informed her that because of the injuries from her automobile accident, it would be unwise for her to attempt to have any more children. Diego agreed firmly with their opinions.

The frescoes he painted in the Detroit Institute of Art were masterpieces of design and accuracy. In them, he compressed vast areas of automobile plants, chemical manufacturing facilities, and other industrial operations into a relatively small space on the museum room's four walls. But the artist took the time to understand the operation of each process before he drew it. Engineers who came to look at the paintings remarked that the machines portrayed were so accurate they should actually work.

Diego Rivera completed his Detroit murals on March 13, 1933. They were officially dedicated—amidst a small army of armed guards and reporters—five days later. Eighty-six thousand people came to see the Rivera frescoes in what was left of the month. Even before the unveiling, however, trouble developed.

Informal art committees began objecting to his pharmacy panel. It showed a nurse holding a child and a doctor giving the child an injection. The panel also included sheep, a horse, and a cow, animals used in the preparation of vaccines. The indignant committees decided that this fresco was the artist's way of mocking the Holy Family of the Christian faith. The child was the baby Jesus, they said, the nurse and doctor were Mary and Joseph, and the animals were from the manger in which Jesus was born.

On March 21, a minister from Detroit's St. Paul's Episcopal Cathedral, the Reverend H. Ralph Higgins, held a meeting in his office attended by various people opposed to the frescoes. Two days after that, a motion was made in Detroit's city council to wash the paintings from the walls. Some councilmen particularly objected to the images of unclothed people in the murals. In an editorial, the *Detroit News* declared: "The best thing to do would be to whitewash the entire work completely."[5] Reverend Higgins went on radio station WXYZ to sound the alarm over the dangers the murals presented.

Opposition to the frescoes continued to mount even after the Riveras left for New York City, where Diego was about to begin his next project. Although a great many civic leaders favored destroying the art, it was saved for two reasons. First, a growing number of people traveled to the museum to see the work for themselves. It was almost impossible to deny the majesty of that work. Second, Edsel Ford finally made a brief speech in support of the paintings. Although his praise was weak, the tepid defense was enough to save the frescoes.

In a magazine article published soon after the Detroit frescoes were unveiled, Rivera suggested that even controversial art would be appreciated by American workers if it had something to do with their lives. He felt that his Detroit murals showed that: "It isn't true that the artistic taste of the North American workers has been created and set by comic strips. . . . If painters insist on creating things that are of no interest to them, then it is only natural that they won't be attracted to them . . . but if they paint things that concern the worker, the response will be immediate."[6]

When Diego and Frida left for New York City late in March 1933, emotions in Detroit were still running out of control. The artist was leaving one controversy behind—and was about to face an even larger one.

For such a rich man, John D. Rockefeller, Jr., had a surprisingly difficult time finding artists willing to decorate the lobby of his new RCA Building in New York. He sent letters and personal messengers to three of the greatest artists of the twentieth century: Pablo Picasso, Henri Matisse, and Diego Rivera. In his communications, the American millionaire asked each artist to submit samples to his precise specifications so that he could choose which he liked best.

It was not a wise way to approach famous artists. Matisse and Rivera sent polite letters turning down the offer to compete. Picasso refused to discuss it. Finally, Rockefeller approached Rivera directly, explaining that the assignment could be his without additional competition. After tedious negotiations, a vague subject and a fee of twenty-one thousand dollars were finally agreed upon. Rivera began work immediately after he arrived in New York City.

"My wall," he said, "standing high above the elevators which faced the main entrance of the building, had already been prepared by my assistants, the scaffold erected, the full-scale sketches traced and stenciled on the wet surface, the colors ground. I painted rapidly and easily. Everything was going smoothly—perhaps too smoothly."[7]

Although he never admitted it, Rivera seemed to be looking for trouble when he chose the subject matter of his Rockefeller Center frescoes. In 1933, America was in the middle of the worst depression in its history. Millions of people, in New York City and across the nation, were out of work. Rockefeller Center, of which the RCA Building was the centerpiece, was being built, in part, to create jobs and improve the economy. Communists throughout the world were using the Depression as proof that they held the only answer to the problems in America and elsewhere. Stung by continuing criticism from his former comrades, Rivera apparently decided to show that he was a good Communist.

In two ellipses crossing at the center of the fresco, Rivera drew scenes depicting the wonders of modern science. To the right, he created cheerful views of life in Communist Russia, including a portrait of Lenin and a May Day celebration in which workers marched and sang. To the left, he showed his disdain for much of Western society. Included in the bleak illustrations were scenes of the idle rich in a nightclub and a view of unemployed workers being attacked by police during a demonstration. Most Americans were sensitive to the economic plight of their nation. Rivera's mural seemed to be rubbing salt into their wounds.

The first big sign of trouble came in a New York newspaper headline on April 24, 1933:

RIVERA PAINTS SCENES OF COMMUNIST

ACTIVITY AND JOHN D. JR. FOOTS BILL[8]

For a time, the Rockefeller family made statements that it supported Rivera's work. But when it became clear that a portrait of Lenin was being included in the fresco, John, Jr., sent a letter asking for its removal.

Apparently, Rivera considered painting out Lenin's portrait. But others around him, especially his assistants, urged against it. Some even threatened to go on strike if the fresco was altered in any way. Finally, Rivera sent Rockefeller a letter suggesting a compromise. To provide balance, the artist would add portraits of some famous Americans, including Abraham Lincoln and John Brown.

"As I awaited Rockefeller's response," Diego remembered, "the hours ticked by in silence. I was seized by a premonition that no further word would come, but that something terrible, instead, was about to happen."[9] As the hours turned to days, armed guards began appearing around the unfinished fresco. Fearing that it would soon be destroyed, Rivera hired a photographer to take pictures of the mural. The guards pushed the photographer away. Finally, one of Rivera's assistants, Lucienne Bloch, managed to take secret photographs of the work with a camera hidden in her blouse.

On the morning of May 9, 1933, a small army of uniformed guards entered the RCA Building lobby and formed a line in front of the fresco. All bystanders were kept away. The artist and his assistants were allowed to continue working in nervous silence. At around dinnertime, when some of his assistants were away, the building's chief architect surrounded by his staff arrived in the lobby. A heavy curtain was pulled across the entrance.

Rivera was called down from his scaffold, presented with a check for his work, and fired. Within minutes, carpenters were at work building a screen to hide the mural from sight. Outside the building, a huge crowd gathered. Included were many people who, before now, had little interest in art. The majority of the demonstrators objected to what was going on inside the locked and curtained building. Police gathered quickly and soon charged the demonstrators. A seven-year-old girl was injured.

More demonstrations were held, some of them quite large. Artists by the dozen sent bitter telegrams to the Rockefellers, many demanding that their works be removed from buildings owned by the wealthy family. Other artists, fewer in number and less well known, expressed their support for Rockefeller's action.

Rivera made a lengthy speech on a New York radio station. "The case of Diego Rivera is a small matter," he said. "I want to explain more clearly the principles involved. Let us take as an example an American millionaire who buys the Sistine Chapel, which contains the works of Michelangelo. . . . Would that millionaire have the right to destroy the Sistine Chapel?"[10]

Rockefeller made a public pledge not to destroy or harm the unfinished frescoes. Instead, he said, they would merely be kept hidden from view. But six months later, at midnight on February 9, 1934, his workers attacked the wall with hammers, pounding the art to bits.

In the meantime, Rivera sought his revenge. His friend and future biographer Bertram D. Wolfe headed an organization called the Communist Party Opposition at the New Worker's school in New York City. The organization, while Communist, was opposed to the mainline Communist views as expressed by Lenin and, more recently, by Joseph Stalin. Wolfe and others invited Rivera to repaint the soon-to-be-destroyed fresco at the New Worker's school.

Realizing that he still had some money left from his work in the RCA Building, Diego was tempted. When he realized that the building was only rented, however, he was worried. "Besides," he said, "it was so old that it was likely soon to fall to the wreckers. Rockefeller would then have the satisfaction of seeing my mural destroyed twice. So I abandoned the idea of reconstructing the Radio City fresco there. But the future pleasure I might have in spending the last of Rockefeller's money to decorate a workers' school struck me as too attractive to forego."[11]

In July 1933, he began work on a series of twenty-one frescoes in the New Worker's school. He placed them on movable frames, so that they would not have to be destroyed along with the old building. The themes of *Portrait of America* are bitter ones, filled with uncomplimentary views of American life, racism, and the struggle of rich against poor. Soon after it was finished, he and Frida returned to Mexico, where they moved into their recently completed home in Mexico City.

The artist's visit in America was filled with controversy, but it made a lasting impression. By the beginning of 1934, President Franklin D. Roosevelt's New Deal program to bring America out of the Great Depression was in full swing. One of his projects involved hiring artists to create murals. Many of the murals painted by Americans under the Public Works of Art Project can still be seen today in government offices, museums, theaters, and other buildings. Few are as memorable, or as controversial, as the works of Diego Rivera.

Chapter 8

GOING HOME

By the time the RCA Building mural was destroyed in February 1934, Diego and Frida were living in their new home in Mexico City. Depressed and in poor health, the artist did little work for several months. In June, he signed a contract to create a smaller version of the destroyed frescoes at a friendlier site: the Palacio de Bellas Artes in Mexico City. Although it was quickly completed, he did no large-scale work until the end of the year. At that time, he started the final frescoes in the still incomplete project at the National Palace.

Remaining to be finished was the large mural entitled *Mexico Today and Tomorrow* at the head of the great stairway. The artist's angry opinion of his country's present and future circumstances was clear when the frescoes were completed late the following year. Labor strikers were shown confronted by soldiers wearing gas masks. Farm organizers faced firing squads. A Communist speaker was shown yelling at a crowd of workers. At the top of the mural, a portrait of Karl Marx was drawn, pointing the way toward Mexico's Communist future.

Before the frescoes were completed, a new president came

to power in Mexico. President Lázaro Cárdenas reformed Mexican law dramatically, helping a vast number of his countrymen obtain their own land for the first time. At approximately the same time, however, the value of Mexican pesos compared with American dollars began to drop severely.

Even for liberal politicians like Cárdenas, Rivera's portrait of civil strife and a Communist future was hard to live with. No one dared destroy his art, but for nine long years, Diego Rivera was offered no public walls to paint in Mexico.

There were other projects, of course, and new controversies as well. With writer Bertram D. Wolfe, he had already published in 1934 a best-selling book entitled *Portrait of America*. Other literary projects with Wolfe were also in the works.

In the summer of 1936, a wealthy politician and art collector named Alberto Pani was building a hotel in Mexico City. In Paris, Pani had once helped Rivera raise money so that the artist could travel to Italy. What better way was there, Pani reasoned, to decorate the Hotel Reforma's banquet room than to hire Diego Rivera for the work? There would be a storm of publicity, of course, which would certainly be noticed by wealthy American tourists visiting Mexico City just as the Hotel Reforma opened.

Rivera accepted the assignment and chose as his theme the carnival of Mexican life. By drawing his carnival, however, the artist managed to land in more hot water. He used the seemingly innocent theme of a folk festival to make bitter comments about Mexican life. The images of well-known politicians and military leaders were shown committing all kinds of rotten acts. In one scene that Rivera himself described, "a pig-faced general danced with a woman symbolizing Mexico; his hand surreptitiously reached over her shoulder to steal fruit from the basket on her back."[1] The drawings were bitter, funny, dangerous, and incredibly embarrassing for the owner of the Hotel Reforma.

In a panic, Pani called in two of his brothers, both architects with painting experience, to make a few changes. Rivera heard about it a few days later.

"Do you know, *maestro*, they have been making alterations in your mural?" a mason asked him.[2] With several friends, Diego rushed to the Hotel Reforma. During the confrontation, guns were waved about and the outraged artist was arrested and forced to spend the night in jail. The last laugh, however, was his. Under Mexican law, the rights of artists were carefully protected. No matter how embarrassing the work might be, the full weight of the law was on the side of Diego Rivera.

Pani was forced to pay two thousand pesos in damages and Rivera was allowed to repair the work. The frescoes, wisely mounted on movable steel frames, were sold a number of times. Today they can be seen on the third floor of the

Museo del Palacio de Bellas Artes in Mexico City.

Due to illnesses as well as his unhealthy political views, Rivera did no mural work for several years. In his autobiography, he told of a number of hair-raising adventures involving Nazi spies, embattled Communist leaders, and Hollywood movie stars that supposedly occurred during this period. Other biographers, particularly Bertram D. Wolfe, question most of them.

Two frightening episodes are undeniable, however. In November 1936, Rivera and Wolfe were sitting together in a Mexican café. With little warning, a government official was shot dead right in front of their eyes. Wolfe wrote that Rivera's "first impulse had been to draw his pistol and intervene, but I thrust him backward from the line of possible cross fire. When it became clear that the body slumped against the wall had suffered immediate death, Diego became calm, except for eager protruding eyes, drinking in, memorizing, fixing forever each detail."[3]

Almost immediately, Rivera began working on a painting about the killing. Wolfe was reminded of another story from Diego's youth, when he and little María had played with the body of their dead baby brother. Some people thought then that Diego acted like a devil. But they misunderstood him. He simply had great calmness in the face of death.

Another violent episode occurred the following year. In 1937, four gunmen walked up to Diego's table at Mexico

City's Restaurant Acapulco. They were preparing to pick a fight and kill him. Frida jumped up in front of her husband and called the four gunmen cowards, demanding to be shot first. She created such a fuss in the restaurant that the attempted assassination became impossible.

"Impossible" was also a good word to describe Frida's relations with Diego. Although she loved him enormously, she also was frustrated that he would not change his unfaithful ways. She soon grew so miserable that Diego insisted on a divorce. In the summer of 1939, they separated and were divorced by the end of the year.

During the brief separation, Diego traveled once again to San Francisco, in the middle of a barrage of publicity. Art was on the minds of many of the city's residents at the time. On artificial Treasure Island in San Francisco Bay, the Golden Gate International Exhibition was in progress. There many artworks by European masters were on display.

Unfortunately, World War II was beginning in Europe at the same time. Anxious European art collectors began recalling their canvases from the American exhibit. Before long, the best-known paintings on Treasure Island had been taken away.

While the Golden Gate International Exhibit was facing ruin, an architect named Timothy Pflueger was designing the buildings for the new City College of San Francisco. Realizing that his city was losing works it had hoped to showcase for two full years, Pflueger had a superb idea. He organized a program called Art in Action, in which artists would create works in full view of Treasure Island visitors. The pieces would later be moved to City College. Great excitement was expressed when it was announced that Diego Rivera had agreed to participate in the program.

Facing a growing threat from Nazi Germany, many Americans began regarding communism as the lesser of two evils. From his point of view, Rivera believed that greater unity was needed among all the Americas to confront the growing power of the Nazis. His mural, he said, "is a symbol of the friendship and common purpose that binds the Americas together."[4]

The huge, exotic mural contained historical scenes from both North America and Latin America. Modern advancements in science and technology also were depicted. Diego worked on the frescoes for as long as the exhibit was open, and for three months afterward. During this period, he talked Frida into coming to San Francisco for medical treatment. They were soon remarried.

Diego's City College of San Francisco frescoes were created, once again, on movable panels. When assembled, the sections made up the largest mural he had ever created outside of Mexico. It was a huge, striking work. Many people felt that the artist at last had made his peace with America.

Diego and Frida Rivera returned to Mexico in January

1942. Four months later, two Mexican ships were destroyed by German submarines. Now Mexico, like most other countries of the world, was drawn into World War II.

During the following war years, Diego created a fresco on two movable panels at the Instituto Nacional de Cardiología (National Institute of Cardiology) in Mexico City. In his fresco, Rivera depicted the history of that important branch of medical science. As he had throughout his life, he continued painting canvases, sometimes in a traditional style, sometimes in a strangely fantastic one.

As he approached his sixtieth birthday, Diego Rivera began to think about his death. As he told Bertram Wolfe, "my father died at seventy-two, my mother at sixty-two, both of cancer. I must die of cancer soon, for I am nearly sixty."[5]

Rivera began designing and constructing a strange building he hoped would serve as both a museum and his tomb. His wife Frida bought a patch of barren land on an ancient lava bed near the city of Coyoacán, just south of Mexico City. On that rocky ground, he made a stone structure that looked more like an ancient ruin than a modern building. He called it Anahuacalli.

Throughout his life, whenever he had money to spare, he had bought ancient stone and clay idols that had been found among the ruins of earlier cultures in Mexico. As the years passed, he assembled approximately sixty thousand pieces of art created before the voyage of Christopher Columbus. It was the largest collection of such art in the world. More than anything else, Anahuacalli became a home for those idols. After his death, he willed the museum and its contents to the people of Mexico.

Fortunately, he had plenty of time to work on the combination museum and tomb. Contrary to his own prediction, the aging artist was far from dead. New walls, and new battles, were just around the corner.

In March 1947, he was hired to paint a mural in a new building, the luxurious Del Prado Hotel. In the hotel dining hall, he painted one of the greatest—and, naturally, most controversial—frescoes of his later years. The hotel was next to Mexico City's large Alameda Park. As a boy, Diego had spent many happy hours exploring that very park.

He called the fresco *Dream of a Sunday Afternoon in Alameda*. "In the center stood I," Diego explained, "a boy of ten, a frog and a snake peering out of my jacket pockets. Beside me, a skeleton in woman's dress held my hand, and my boyhood master, José Guadalupe Posada, famous for his drawings of skeletons, held her other hand under his arm. Frida, as a grown woman, stood behind me, her hand on my shoulder. On the right side of the mural, I also painted Lupe Marín beside our two adult daughters. Above them were portraits of historical figures representing the social classes of Mexico."[6]

The dream included typical scenes from a park as well as events from Mexican and world history. The strange and beautiful fresco was huge: nearly fifty feet long and sixteen feet high. On all of this vast space, a tiny area just two inches high caused yet another scandal for Diego Rivera

There, in relatively small but unmistakable letters, were the words "God does not exist." It was actually a quotation once made by a historical figure, but that fact was lost on everyone who saw it. A Catholic archbishop refused to bless the new hotel until the entire mural was covered up. A mob of young students stormed the hotel, slashing the portrait of young Diego and scratching out the offending words. They continued marching to the Riveras' studio in San Angel and the stone building called Anahuacalli, smashing windows at both sites.

The riots at last died down. But for nine years, *Dream of a Sunday Afternoon in Alameda* remained hidden behind a screen in the Del Prado Hotel. Occasionally, the barrier would be removed for interested visitors, and then quickly put back in place.

By the late summer of 1949, the controversy had been all but forgotten. Now Mexico began celebrating a full fifty years of work by Diego Rivera with a huge exhibit. More than a thousand of his artworks were borrowed from collectors from all over the world, including the Nelson Rockefellers and the widow of John D. Rockefeller, Jr. Opening the exhibit in August, Mexican president Miguel Alemán Valdés called the artist a "national treasure."[7]

By the early 1950s, both Diego and Frida encountered growing health problems. Now well into his sixties, Diego found painting more difficult.

But Mexico's "national treasure" could still use his art to create a few more scandals. In February 1952, he painted a picture called *The Nightmare of War and the Dream of Peace* as part of a large exhibition of Mexican art. Made in little more than a month, the huge painting was of poor quality. But the political content enraged many people. It showed Joseph Stalin, the ruthless premier of Russia, standing next to Mao Tse-tung, the leader of Communist China, holding a peace treaty. Among the people facing them was Uncle Sam, a familiar symbol of the United States.

With a machine gun slung over his shoulder, Uncle Sam held a Bible in one hand and a bundle of cash in the other. At the time, the United States was involved in a war, helping the people of South Korea fight against the people of North Korea. Rivera's painting showed South Korean soldiers killing and whipping North Koreans. Just to be sure no one missed his message, he included an African-American nailed to the cross.

The Nightmare of War and the Dream of Peace was an attack on the United States and a defense of the Communist governments in the U.S.S.R. and China. It also was bad art, carelessly drawn even for an artist with Diego's worsening health.

But its purpose was clear a few months later. Long ago expelled from the Communist party of Mexico, Rivera was seeking to become a member once again. In the hope of doing so, he became what he once complained about: a propaganda painter. As he well knew, propaganda art needed only to convey the ideas of Communist leaders. It didn't have to be good. He hoped that his attempt at creating party-line propaganda would help get him back into the party. But at the end of 1952, his application was turned down.

A year and a half later, on July 13, 1954, his wife Frida died. Although Diego seemed to oppose it, her funeral was turned into a Communist demonstration. "I was oblivious to it all," Diego sadly recalled. "July 13, 1954, was the most tragic day of my life. I had lost my beloved Frida forever."[8] Two months later, the Communist party of Mexico finally accepted him as a member once again. In truth, Diego Rivera was a better Communist than the Communist party deserved.

Comrade Rivera painted a number of other Communist propaganda pieces. Most were of poor quality. But even in his last years, he showed that his skills remained sharp. A number of his simple portraits, especially one drawn of a Mexican art collector named Dolores Olmedo, were of excellent quality and extremely popular.

On July 29, 1955, he married a Mexican art dealer named Emma Hurtado. For nearly a decade, Emma had sold his paintings at a Mexico City gallery. Just before his marriage, however, he was diagnosed as having cancer. He continued with the marriage and continued working. In August, he made a final visit to Russia, where he was given radiation treatments for his cancer. Announcing that he was entirely cured, he made a brief tour of Eastern European nations before returning to Mexico on April 4, 1956.

In Mexico, he felt he had one important duty remaining. Nine days after his return, he climbed weakly onto a specially prepared scaffold in the dining hall of the Hotel del Prado. From the mural he had painted nine years earlier, he removed the words "God does not exist." At a press conference two days later, he stunned reporters by saying, "I am a Catholic." He also said, "It is my desire to gratify my countrymen, the Mexican Catholics, who comprise 96 per cent of the population of the country."[9]

The next year was his last. On November 24, 1957, he died of heart failure at the age of seventy in his studio.

Near the end of Rivera's life, his renewed Communist activities caused great embarrassment in Detroit. Members of the city council once again considered removing or destroying the frescoes he created there. In response to pointed questions from councilmen, the Detroit Art Commission made the following written report:

"We regret that Rivera's present behavior has revived the old controversy. There is no question that Rivera enjoys making trouble. . . . But this man, who often behaves like a child, is one of the outstanding talents of the Western Hemisphere. . . . In the Detroit frescoes we have one of the best as well as one of the most serious of his works. No other artist in the world could have painted murals of such magnitude and force. . . . We recommend that the paintings remain on exhibition."[10]

As a human being, Diego Rivera was charming, infuriating, unpredictable, and complex. He was a totally unfaithful husband who inspired both praise and scorn from nearly every woman in his life. As a political philosopher, he was brave, stimulating, and shallow. As an artist, he was a genius.

Diego Rivera is gone now, but the world should have a long, long time to consider his art. Cast in a material that is almost like stone, his paintings will probably last for generations to come.

Diego Rivera 1886-1957

1886 Diego Rivera is born. The Statue of Liberty is dedicated. The eighth and last impressionist exhibition is held in Paris. Steam is used to sterilize surgical instruments. The Canadian Pacific Railway is completed.

1887 Queen Victoria of England celebrates her golden jubilee. Sir Arthur Conan Doyle publishes the first Sherlock Holmes story. The sound quality of the phonograph is improved. Thomas Alva Edison and Sir Joseph Wilson Swan combine to produce Ediswan electric lamps.

1888 Benjamin Harrison is elected president of the United States. George Eastman perfects the Kodak box camera. John Boyd Dunlap invents the pneumatic tire. The Football League and the Lawn Tennis Association are founded.

1889 North Dakota, South Dakota, Montana, and Washington become states of the United States. Charlie Chaplin is born. Alexander-Gustave Eiffel designs a 984-foot-high tower for the Paris World Exhibition.

1890 Idaho and Wyoming become states. The first moving-picture shows appear in the United States. Paul Cézanne paints *The Card Players*. The first entirely steel framed building is erected in Chicago.

1891 The painter Paul Gauguin settles in Tahiti. Henri Toulouse-Lautrec produces his first music-hall posters. Wireless telegraphy is invented. Construction begins on the Trans-Siberian Railroad.

1892 The Rivera family move to Mexico City. Grover Cleveland is elected president of the United States. Claude Monet begins his series of pictures on the Rouen Cathedral. Rudolf Diesel patents his internal-combustion engine. The first automatic telephone switchboard is introduced.

1893 Hawaii is proclaimed a republic and is annexed by treaty to the United States. "Art Nouveau" appears in Paris. Karl Benz constructs his four-wheeled car. A World Exhibition is held in Chicago.

1894 French army captain Alfred Dreyfuss is arrested on treason charges, convicted, and sent to Devil's Island, French Guiana. Louis Lumière invents the cinematograph.

1895 Cuba fights Spain for its independence. Abraham Roentgen discovers X rays. Guglielmo Marconi invents radio telegraphy. Auguste and Louis Lumière invent a motion-picture camera. King Camp Gillette invents the safety razor. The first professional football game is played in the U.S.

1896 Rivera enrolls in night classes at the San Carlos School of Fine Arts. Utah becomes a state. William McKinley is elected president of the U.S. Five annual Nobel prizes are established for those who have conferred the greatest benefits on mankind in the fields of physics, physiology and medicine, chemistry, literature, and peace. The first modern Olympics are held in Athens, Greece.

1897 There is a World Exhibition in Brussels, Belgium. A Zionist congress is held in Basel, Switzerland. Queen Victoria celebrates her diamond jubilee.

1898 Rivera is graduated from elementary school with honors. He completes a pencil drawing entitled *Head of a Woman*. U.S. declares war on Spain over Cuba. The first photographs using artificial light are taken.

1899 The Philippines demand independence from the U.S. The Boers are defeated in South Africa. Ernst Pringsheim and Otto Lummer undertake important radiation studies.

1900 McKinley is reelected president. The Boxer Rebellions against Europeans take place in China.

The cakewalk is the most fashionable dance. There is a World Exhibition in Paris.

1901 President McKinley is assassinated by an anarchist and is succeeded by Theodore Roosevelt. Cuba becomes a U.S. protectorate. Pablo Picasso enters his "Blue Period." Ragtime jazz is popular in the U.S. The first British submarine is launched.

1902 Francis Bacon becomes the first man to cross the Irish Channel in a balloon. The United States assumes control over the Panama Canal. In Egypt, the Aswan Dam is opened. The singer Enrico Caruso makes his first phonograph recording.

1903 A 12-minute film, *The Great Train Robbery*, is the longest to date. Willem Einthoven invents the electrocardiogram. Richard Stieff designs the first teddy bear. Henry Ford designs the Ford Motor car.

1904 Teddy Roosevelt is elected president. William Gorgas eradicates yellow fever in Panama. Work begins on the Panama Canal. War breaks out between Russia and China. A tunnel is built under the Hudson River between New York and New Jersey.

1905 The first regular cinema is established in Pittsburgh. Albert Einstein formulates the theory of relativity. Rayon yarn is manufactured commercially. The first motor buses appear in London. The first neon light signs appear.

1906 President Porfirio Díaz orders cruel attacks on Mexican striking workers. U.S. troops occupy Cuba. President Roosevelt, on the first trip outside the U.S. by a president, visits the Canal Zone in Panama. Roald Amundsen, a Norwegian explorer, crosses the Northwest Passage and determines the position of the North Pole. An earthquake in San Francisco kills 3,000 people.

1907 Rivera goes to Spain. A panic in the U.S. causes a run on banks. The first cubist exhibition is held in Paris. Lumière develops a process for color photography. The *Lusitania* sails from Ireland to New York in five days. The first modern zoo is opened in Hamburg, Germany. Mother's Day is established.

1908 The Union of South Africa is established. William Howard Taft is elected president of the U.S. The first steel and glass building is built in Berlin, Germany. Fountain pens become popular. Wilbur Wright flies 30 miles in 40 minutes. The Ford Motor Company produces the Model T.

1909 Rivera visits Paris, where he lives and works for the next ten years. Rivera meets Angeline Belloff. He completes his painting, *The House on the Bridge*. U.S. explorer Robert E. Peary reaches the North Pole. Halley's comet is observed.

1910 Rivera returns to Mexico where his art is exhibited in Mexico City; many of his paintings are sold. There is a revolution in Mexico against the long Díaz dictatorship. In the U.S., Frank Lloyd Wright becomes well known for his domestic architecture.

1911 Rivera returns to Paris where he and Angeline begin living together. Armistice ends the Mexican civil war. Amundsen reaches the South Pole. Charles F. Kettering develops the first practical electric self-starter for automobiles.

1912 Arizona and New Mexico become states. Woodrow Wilson is elected president of the U.S. The S.S. *Titanic* sinks on her maiden voyage. The first successful parachute jump takes place.

1913 Rivera becomes one of the leaders of a new movement called cubism. A federal income tax is introduced in the U.S. through the Sixteenth Amendment. Grand Central Terminal opens in New York City. The dance called the fox-trot comes into fashion.

1914 Rivera's first one-man show is held in Paris. World War I begins. The Panama Canal is opened. The first heart surgery is performed on a dog. The Lincoln Memorial in Washington, D.C. is designed.

1915 Rivera paints *Zapatista Landscape—The Guerrilla*. World War I continues. New Orleans jazz is in bloom. Albert Einstein postulates his general theory of relativity. A transcontinental phone call is made between Alexander Graham Bell in New York and Dr. Thomas A. Watson in San Francisco.

1916 Rivera's son. Diego, Jr., is born on August 11. Wilson is reelected president. Francisco "Pancho" Villa, Mexican revolutionary general, crosses the border with guerrillas and raids Columbus, New Mexico, killing 17 Americans. Blood for transfusions is refrigerated. An underwater ultrasonic source for submarine detection is developed.

1917 In Mexico land reform and a more democratic constitution are achieved. Rivera stops painting in the cubist style. Chicago becomes the world's jazz center. The first baseball game is played on a Sunday at the Polo Grounds in New York City.

1918 Diego Rivera, Jr., dies. Wilson puts forth his Fourteen Points for world peace. An armistice ending World War I is signed between the Allies and Germany. Daylight Saving Time is introduced in America. Regular airmail service is established between New York and Washington.

1919 Prohibition, the Eighteenth Amendment to the U.S. Constitution, is ratified. President Wilson presides over the first League of Nations meeting in Paris. Jazz arrives in Europe. The first experiments with shortwave radio are carried out.

1920 Rivera goes to Italy to study frescoes. The U.S. Senate votes against joining the League of Nations. Warren G. Harding is elected president of the U.S.

1921 Rivera returns to Paris and then to Mexico. Britain and Ireland sign a peace treaty. The northern approaches to Mount Everest are explored by a British team. The first radio broadcast of a baseball game is made from the Polo Grounds in New York. The Unknown Soldier is interred at Arlington National Cemetery. The Ku Klux Klan becomes violent throughout the southern states.

1922 Rivera paints murals at the University of Mexico. Rivera and Guadalupe "Lupe" Marín are wed. Italian Benito Mussolini forms Fascist government. Insulin is first administered to diabetic patients. Concrete tennis courts are opened at Wimbledon, England.

1923 Lee de Forest demonstrates a process for sound motion pictures. An Argentine swimmer, Enrique Tiroboschi, crosses the English Channel in 16 hours, 33 minutes. Moritz Schick patents the electric razor.

1924 Calvin Coolidge is elected president of the U.S. The World Chess League is founded at The Hague, The Netherlands. In the U.S., 2.5 million radios are in use.

1925 Nellie Ross of Wyoming becomes the first woman governor. A Scottish inventor, John Baird, transmits human features by television. John T. Scopes, a schoolteacher, goes on trial for violating Tennessee law that prohibits the teaching of the theory of evolution; he is defended by Clarence Darrow.

1926 Rivera and Lupe are separated (and later divorced). Fascist youth organizations are formed in Germany and Italy. The "Electrola," a new electric recording technique, is developed. Kodak produces the first 16-mm movie film. Alan Cobham flies from England to Capetown, South Africa, to investigate the feasibility of long-distance air routes. A cushioned, cork-centered baseball is introduced.

1927 Rivera goes to Moscow, U.S.S.R. Charles A. Lindbergh flies his monoplane, *The Spirit of St. Louis*. The slow fox-trot becomes a fashionable dance. Babe Ruth hits 60 home runs for the

New York Yankees. The Great Moffat Tunnel through the Rocky Mountains is opened.

1928 Rivera returns to Mexico and is thrown out of the Communist party. Herbert Hoover is elected president of the U.S. Amelia Earhart is the first woman to fly across the Atlantic. The first television broadcasts are scheduled in Schenectady, New York. The first Mickey Mouse films are issued. The first color motion pictures are exhibited by George Eastman in Rochester, New York.

1929 Rivera is married to Frida Kahlo. He is named director of San Carlos School of Fine Arts. U.S. aviator Richard A. Byrd and three companions fly over the South Pole. "Black Friday" in New York—the U.S. Stock Exchange collapses, the beginning of the Great Depression. The Bell Laboratories experiment with the first color television. Kodak introduces 16-mm color film. In the St. Valentine's Day Massacre, six notorious Chicago gangsters are machine-gunned to death by a rival gang.

1930 Rivera is ousted from director's office at San Carlos School of Fine Arts. He completes murals in the National Palace in Mexico City. Contract bridge becomes a popular card game. The photoflash bulb comes into use. Comic strips grow in popularity in the U.S. A yellow-fever vaccine is developed.

1931 Rivera paints murals in San Francisco. The Museum of Modern Art in New York City has a one-man show of Rivera's work. The northern face of the Matterhorn is climbed for the first time. The first trans-African railroad line is completed. The Empire State Building and the George Washington Bridge in New York are completed.

1932 Rivera (with Frida) goes to Detroit to plan work for Detroit Institute of Art. Franklin D. Roosevelt is elected president of the U.S. Amelia Earhart flies solo across the Atlantic in 13.5 hours. The term "New Deal" is used by Roosevelt for the first time. Auguste Picard reaches a height of 17.5 miles in his stratospheric balloon. Work begins on the Golden Gate Bridge between San Francisco and Oakland.

1933 Rivera's murals in Detroit are completed and dedicated amid controversy; Rivera and Frida go to New York City. Rivera paints frescoes in Rockefeller Center that include portrait of Lenin and a May Day celebration. Adolf Hitler is appointed chancellor of Germany and is granted dictatorial powers. The first concentration camps are erected in Germany. American banks are closed from March 6 to 9 to stem the tide of bank failures. Philo Farnsworth develops electronic television. The Chicago World's Fair opens. The Twenty-first Amendment to the U.S. Constitution repeals Prohibition.

1934 Rivera's frescoes in Radio City, New York, are vandalized. Hitler and Mussolini meet in Venice, Italy. A refrigeration process for meat cargoes is devised. W. Beebe descends 3,028 feet into the ocean off Bermuda. The S.S. *Normandie* is launched—the largest ship afloat.

1935 President Roosevelt signs the U.S. Social Security Act. Radar equipment to detect aircraft is built. The first sulfa drug for treating streptococcal infections is developed. The rumba becomes a fashionable dance.

1936 Rivera paints murals for the Hotel Reforma in Mexico City. German troops occupy the Rhineland. Mussolini and Hitler proclaim the Rome-Berlin Axis. Roosevelt is reelected president of the U.S. by a landslide. BBC/London inaugurates television service. The Spanish Civil War begins.

1937 Wall Street stock market decline signals serious economic recession in U.S. Royal Commission of Palestine recommends establishment of Arab and Jewish states. Nylon is patented by the Du Pont Company. Amelia Earhart is lost on a Pacific flight. The disaster involving the dirigible

Hindenburg at Lakehurst, New Jersey, is described in the first transcontinental radio broadcast. The first jet engine is built.

1938   Hitler appoints himself war minister. Germany annexes Czechoslovakia. Roosevelt appeals to Hitler and Mussolini to settle European problems amicably. The ballpoint pen is invented. The S.S. *Queen Elizabeth* is launched.

1939   Rivera and Frida Kahlo are divorced. The Spanish Civil War ends. Germany invades Poland. Britain and France declare war on Germany. U.S. economy begins to recover and is booming from orders for arms and war equipment. Pan American Airlines begins regular scheduled flights between Europe and the U.S. World War II begins in Europe.

1940   Germany invades Norway and Denmark. The Battle of Britain begins. Roosevelt is elected for a third term. Penicillin is developed as an antibiotic. The first electron microscope is demonstrated.

1941   Rivera paints frescoes for City College of San Francisco. The Japanese attack Pearl Harbor. U.S. and Britain declare war on Japan. U.S. declares war on Germany and Italy. The National Gallery of Art opens in Washington, D.C. The "Manhattan Project" of intensive atomic research begins.

1942   Rivera and Frida remarry. The murder of millions of Jews in Nazi gas chambers begins. The first automatic computer is developed in the U.S. "Magnetic recording" tape is invented.

1943   World War II continues on two fronts. President Roosevelt freezes wages, salaries, and prices to forestall inflation. Pay-as-you-go income-tax system is instituted in the U.S. Race riots break out in several major cities in the U.S. whose labor population has seen an influx of Southern blacks.

1944   D-Day: Allies land in Normandy. Americans capture Guam from the Japanese. Roosevelt is reelected for a fourth term. The first nonstop flight takes place from London to Canada.

1945   Roosevelt dies and is succeeded by Harry S. Truman. V.E. Day ends the war in Europe. The United Nations (UN) charter is signed in San Francisco. U.S. drops atomic bombs on Hiroshima and Nagasaki, Japan. Japan surrenders. World War II ends.

1946   The UN General Assembly holds its first session in London. New York is declared the site of its permanent headquarters. Xerography is invented. A pilotless rocket missile is constructed by the Fairey Aviation Company.

1947   Rivera paints a mural in the Del Prado Hotel in Mexico City entitled *Dream of a Sunday Afternoon in Alameda*. A British proposal to divide Palestine is rejected by Arabs and Jews; the question is referred to the UN, which announces a plan for partition. India is declared independent and is partitioned into India and Pakistan. The first U.S. airplane flies at supersonic speeds. Bell Laboratories scientists invent the transistor.

1948   The Jewish State of Israel come into existence. Truman is elected president of the U.S. The long-playing record is invented.

1949   Chaing Kai-shek resigns as president of China—the Communist People's Republic is proclaimed. Israel is admitted to the UN. Cortisone is discovered. The state of Vietnam is established.

1950   Truman instructs the U.S. Atomic Energy Commission to develop the hydrogen bomb. North Korea invades South Korea. Miltown comes into wide use as a tranquilizer. Antihistamines become popular remedies for colds and allergies.

1951   The Twenty-second Amendment to the U.S. Constitution is passed, providing for a maximum of two terms for U.S. presidents. A heart-lung machine for heart operations is developed. Color television is introduced in the U.S.

1952 Rivera's painting, *The Nightmare of War and the Dream of Peace*, arouses great controversy, as an attack on U.S. and defense of communism. Dwight D. Eisenhower is elected president. Anti-British riots erupt in Egypt. The first hydrogen bomb is exploded at Eniwetok Atoll in the Pacific. The S.S. *United States* crosses the Atlantic in 3 days and 10 hours.

1953 In the U.S. the Rosenbergs, sentenced as atomic spies in 1951, are executed. The Korean War ends. Sir Edmund Hillary and Tenzing Norgay are the first to climb Mt. Everest. Lung cancer is reported attributable to cigarette smoking.

1954 Frida Kahlo dies. U.S. Supreme Court rules that segregation by color in public schools is a violation of the Fourteenth Amendment. Dr. Jonas Salk begins innoculating Pittsburgh children with a polio vaccine.

1955 Rivera weds Emma Hurtado. Blacks in Montgomery, Alabama, boycott segregated city bus lines. Raids on Israel-Jordan border increase. Atomically generated power is first used in the U.S. at Schenectady, New York.

1956 Dwight D. Eisenhower is reelected president of the U.S. Soviet troops march into Hungary. Martin Luther King, Jr., emerges as leader of campaign for desegregation. Albert Sabin develops an oral polio vaccine.

1957 Diego Rivera dies. Israeli forces withdraw from Sinai Peninsula and hand over Gaza Strip to UN forces. U.S.S.R. launches *Sputnik I* and *Sputnik II*, the first earth satellites. A desegregation crisis develops in Little Rock, Arkansas. President Eisenhower sends in paratroopers to forestall violence.

ACKNOWLEDGMENTS

The editors would like to acknowledge use of excerpted material from the following works:

Copyright © 1963 by Bertram Wolfe, from the book THE FABULOUS LIFE OF DIEGO RIVERA, originally published by Stein & Day, Inc., reprinted with permission of Scarborough House Publishers.

My Art, My Life, Diego Rivera with Gladys March, Copyright © 1960 by Gladys Stevens March, published by the Citadel Press. Used by permission.

DIEGO RIVERA: THE SHAPING OF AN ARTIST: 1889-1921 by Florence Arquin, copyright © 1971 by the University of Oklahoma Press.

Arte y politica/Diego Rivera, ed. Raquel Tibol, copyright © 1979, published by Editorial Grijalbo.

Diego Rivera, A Retrospective, ed. Cynthia Newman Helms, copyright © 1986 by Founders Society Detroit Institute of Arts, published by W.W. Norton & Co., Inc.

NOTES

Chapter 1
1. Bertram D. Wolfe, *The Fabulous Life of Diego Rivera* (New York: Stein and Day, 1963): 16
2. Diego Rivera (with Gladys March), *My Art, My Life* (New York: The Citadel Press, 1960): 19
3. Ibid., 20-21
4. Florence Arquin, *Diego Rivera: The Shaping of an Artist, 1889-1921* (Norman, Oklahoma: University of Oklahoma Press, 1971): 7
5. Rivera (with Gladys March), *My Art, My Life*: 23-24
6. Ibid., 24-25
7. Ibid., 28

Chapter 2
1. Bertram D. Wolfe, *The Fabulous Life of Diego Rivera*: 21
2. Ibid.
3. Diego Rivera (with Gladys March), *My Art, My Life*: 22
4. Wolfe, *The Fabulous Life of Diego Rivera*: 28
5. Rivera (with Gladys March), *My Art, My Life*: 32-33
6. Ibid., 41
7. Florence Arquin, *Diego Rivera: The Shaping of an Artist, 1889-1921*: 18
8. Rivera (with Gladys March), *My Art, My Life*: 40

Chapter 3
1. Diego Rivera (with Gladys March), *My Art, My Life*: 48
2. Ibid., 49
3. Ibid., 52
4. Bertram D. Wolfe, *The Fabulous Life of Diego Rivera*: 47
5. Rivera (with Gladys March), *My Art, My Life*: 52
6. Ibid., 56
7. Florence Arquin, *Diego Rivera: The Shaping of an Artist, 1889-1921*: 61
8. Rivera (with Gladys March), *My Art, My Life*: 65
9. Ibid., 67
10. Ibid., 71-72
11. Ibid., 86

Chapter 4
1. Diego Rivera (with Gladys March), *My Art, My Life*: 102
2. Florence Arquin, *Diego Rivera: The Shaping of an Artist, 1889-1921*: 87-88
3. Rivera (with Gladys March), *My Art, My Life*: 106-7
4. Ibid., 107
5. Bertram D. Wolfe, *The Fabulous Life of Diego Rivera*: 99
6. Rivera (with Gladys March), *My Art, My Life*: 119-20
7. Ibid., 120
8. Ibid., 121-22

Chapter 5
1. Bertram D. Wolfe, *The Fabulous Life of Diego Rivera*: 121
2. Diego Rivera (with Gladys March), *My Art, My Life*: 124
3. Ibid., 127
4. Ibid., 130
5. Ibid., 133
6. Ibid., 134
7. Wolfe, *The Fabulous Life of Diego Rivera*: 181
8. Rivera (with Gladys March), *My Art, My Life*: 135-36
9. Wolfe, *The Fabulous Life of Diego Rivera*: 202-3
10. Ibid., 192

Chapter 6
1. Diego Rivera (with Gladys March), *My Art, My Life*: 145
2. Bertram D. Wolfe, *The Fabulous Life of Diego Rivera*: 221

3. Raquel Tibol (ed.), *Arte y politicia/Diego Rivera* (Mexico City: Editorial Grijalbo, 1979): 27
4. Rivera (with Gladys March), *My Art, My Life*: 161
5. Ibid., 158
6. *The New York Times*, August 23, 1929. Quoted in Bertram D. Wolfe, *The Fabulous Life of Diego Rivera*: 248
7. Wolfe, *The Fabulous Life of Diego Rivera*: 243
8. Ibid., 244
9. Rivera (with Gladys March), *My Art, My Life*: 175

Chapter 7
1. Diego Rivera (with Gladys March), *My Art, My Life*: 183
2. Ibid., 186
3. Ibid., 188
4. Bertram D. Wolfe, *The Fabulous Life of Diego Rivera*: 309
5. Ibid., 313
6. Rivera, "Art and the Worker," *The Modern Monthly* (June 1933)
7. Rivera (with Gladys March), *My Art, My Life*: 204
8. Joseph Lilly writing in the *New York World-Telegram*, April 24, 1933; quoted in Bertram D. Wolfe, *The Fabulous Life of Diego Rivera*: 324
9. Rivera (with Gladys March), *My Art, My Life*: 207
10. Wolfe, *The Fabulous Life of Diego Rivera*: 330

11. Rivera (with Gladys March), *My Art, My Life*: 211

Chapter 8
1. Diego Rivera (with Gladys March), *My Art, My Life*: 217
2. Bertram D. Wolfe, *The Fabulous Life of Diego Rivera*: 351
3. Ibid., 28
4. From an unidentified newspaper clipping in the San Francisco Main Library; quoted in a footnote to "Mural Census: City College of San Francisco," as published in *Diego Rivera: A Retrospective*, Founders Society Detroit Institute of Arts (New York: W.W. Norton & Co., Inc., 1986): 335
5. Wolfe, *The Fabulous Life of Diego Rivera*: 367
6. Rivera (with Gladys March), *My Art, My Life*: 254
7. Laurance P. Hurlburt, "Diego Rivera (1886-1957): A Chronology of His Art, Life, and Times," as published in *Diego Rivera: A Retrospective*, Founders Society Detroit Institute of Arts (New York: W.W. Norton & Co., Inc., 1986): 107
8. Rivera (with Gladys March), *My Art, My Life*: 285
9. Wolfe, *The Fabulous Life of Diego Rivera*: 409
10. Ibid., 390

INDEX- *Page numbers in boldface type indicate illustrations.*

About the Author

Jim Hargrove has worked as a writer and editor for more than ten years. After serving as an editorial director for three Chicago area publishers, he began a career as an independent writer, preparing a series of books for children. He has contributed to works by nearly twenty different publishers. His Childrens Press titles include biographies of Mark Twain, Daniel Boone, Thomas Jefferson, Lyndon B. Johnson, Steven Spielberg, Nelson Mandela, and Richard Nixon. With his wife and daughter, he lives in a small Illinois town near the Wisconsin border.